BRITISH STEAM
PAST AND PRESENT

BRITISH STEAM

PAST AND PRESENT

Keith Langston

WHARNCLIFFE
TRANSPORT

First published in Great Britain in 2009 by
Mortons Media Group Ltd

Reprinted in this format in 2011 by
Wharncliffe Transport
an imprint of
Pen and Sword Books Limited,
47 Church Street, Barnsley,
South Yorkshire, S70 2AS

ISBN: 978 1 84468 122 8

A CIP catalogue record of this book is available from the
British Library.

Printed in China through
Printworks lnt. Ltd.

Pen & Sword Books Ltd incorporates the imprints of
Pen & Sword Aviation, Pen & Sword Maritime,
Pen & Sword Military, Wharncliffe Local History, Pen & Sword Select,
Pen & Sword Military Classics, Leo Cooper, Remember When,
Seaforth Publishing and Frontline Publishing

For a complete list of Pen & Sword titles please contact:
PEN & SWORD BOOKS LIMITED
47 Church Street, Barnsley, South Yorkshire, S70 2AS, England.
E-mail: enquiries@pen-and-sword.co.uk
Website: www.pen-and-sword.co.uk

CONTENTS

INTRODUCTION

British Steam: Past and Present celebrates the glory of steam railway locomotives. This publication contains an evocative mix of specially commissioned modern steam images and archive pictures, the majority of which have never been published before.

The rebuild of ex LMS No 6100 Royal Scot, and the history of the class are covered in depth, including the facts about 'which Scot went to the USA'. The building of loco No 60163 Tornado is featured, together with a look back at the powerful ex LNER/BR Peppercorn 'A1' Class.

British steam new build projects continue to forge ahead, accordingly the ex LMS Patriot Class is highlighted as is the building of new locomotive No 45551 The Unknown Warrior.

The 'Steam Era' is brought into focus with unique 1950s and 60s archive pictures from Beattock, Oxford and the Belfast-Dublin ex GNR (Ireland) route.

Preserved steam action includes images from the 'Bluebell Railway', the 'Churnet Valley Railway', the 'UK Main Line' and the Great Central Railway. Together with many archive pictures from the author's own collection this publication presents an enthralling 'window on steam'. The high quality print style and relaxed format allows pictures to be used as the photographer intended them to be, thus creating an impressive record of 'British Steam Power'.

Keith Langston.

'Fresh out of the works'. Ex LMS/BR rebuilt 'Scot' 4-6-0 number 6100 *Royal Scot* is pictured during a steaming test at the works of LNWR Heritage, Crewe on Thursday 19 March 2009. Author

Chapter I

THE LEDENDARY 'ROYAL SCOT' CLASS

Two examples of the engine class many consider to have been the finest express steam locomotives of their time have now been restored to running order, No 6115 *Scots Guardsman* in 2008 and the class leader No 6100 *Royal Scot* just over a year later. The former by the restoration team at West Coast Railway Co Ltd, who also own and regularly operate No 6115 from their WCML-connected Carnforth depot and the latter, formerly resident at Bressingham Steam Museum, by first a dedicated team at Southall Restoration Centre, and then by Pete Waterman's Crewe-based London & North Western Railway Heritage Co Ltd.

Sir Henry Fowler

In 1927 the LMS found itself in urgent need of powerful express locomotives to replace the ageing and somewhat under-powered Claughton Class on its heavier Anglo Scottish services. Having been impressed with a GWR 4-6-0 'Castle Class' locomotive (No 5000 *Launceston Castle*) during a 1926 locomotive exchange, the London Midland & Scottish Railways Chief Mechanical Engineer Sir Henry Fowler (1925-1931) allegedly asked Swindon to build 50 'Castle' types for the LMS.

History has it that the GWR chiefs declined to accept the order and even put a block on Swindon lending the Derby design office a set of 'King Class' drawings! Thus the only alternative open to Fowler was to design his own three-cylinder 4-6-0. Maunsell of the Southern Railway lent a hand and sanctioned the loan of a set of 'Lord Nelson Class' drawings to Derby and whether the drawings were useful or not is open to debate.

The LMS were from several accounts impressed with the performance of the four-cylinder 'Nelsons' but in the event decided to proceed with their original plans to build a three-cylinder loco. Hence the Royal Scot Class was born. After the completion of the design work at Derby the order for the first 50 locos was placed, not with an LMS works but with the contractors North British Locomotive Co Ltd of Glasgow.

Building the Royal Scot Class

The loco currently under restoration is one of two survivors from a class of 71 locomotives built to a Midland Railway Fowler design at North British Locomotive Co Ltd Glasgow (50 locos plus No 6399 rebuild) and LMS Derby Works (20 locos). The loco now considered to be No 6100 Royal Scot is from the Derby batch, the other surviving rebuilt 'Royal Scot Class' loco being No 6115 *Scots Guardsman* (No 46115) an NBL-built example.

The first of the Royal Scot Class was outshopped on 14 August 1927 by North British Locomotive Co Ltd as No 6100 Royal Scot; the last loco of the class was

Unrebuilt Royal Scot 4-6-0 No 46148 *The Manchester Regiment* (named *Velocipede* until 1935) pictured with a Glasgow Central-Birmingham New Street express at Carstairs station on 4 July 1953. Loco No 46148 was built by NBL (a Hyde Park engine) and entered LMS service in November 1927, being withdrawn by BR in November 1964, having run in the region of 1.4 million miles in service. David Anderson

LMS poster of the era, depicting loco No 6136 *The Border Regiment*, a loco built by NBL (Hyde Park engine) in September 1927. Author's Collection

built in November 1930 by Derby Works. The class total includes the former experimental high pressure loco No 6399 *Fury* which was rebuilt as a Royal Scot by NBL Ltd in 1935, thereafter taken into service with the LMS number 6170 and named *British Legion*.

There was a growing and urgent need for the new locomotives and so to expedite matters North British Locomotive Co Ltd split the construction work between two manufacturing centres. Under order L.833 Queens Park Works (the old Dubs factory close to Polmadie depot) was tasked with building 25 locos while order L.834 called for 25 engines to be built at Hyde Park Works (the old Neilson Reid erecting shops). The first 50 'Scots' were given LMSR running numbers 6100-6149 of which 6100-6124 (NBL works numbers 23595-23619) were Queens Park Engines and 6125-6149 (NBL works numbers 23620-23644) Hyde Park engines.

The first Royal Scot identity switch

Enthusiasts at the time were a little bemused by the goings on at NBL, as they eagerly awaited sight of the first new engine. Every effort was made to ensure that one engine was completed as soon as possible and that was the first engine produced at Queens Park, No 6100. However the first completed Hyde Park engine No 6125 was painted in shop grey, complemented by an LMSR crest on the cab side, 6100 in large numerals on the tender side and then used for the official photograph.

Eagle-eyed enthusiasts spotted what they realised was an error in the simulation. The loco photographed as No 6100 carried a circular-shaped Hyde Park works plate on the smokebox side with the correct NBL works number (23593) for 6100. But the observers noticed that the plate should have been in the style of Queens Park works, and therefore diamond shaped, not circular! The inaccuracy was corrected before the 'real' 6100 *Royal Scot* was delivered by the NBL to the LMSR at Polmadie Depot, Glasgow, and thereafter loco No 6125 reverting to its own identity.

Top quality locos at a bargain price!

Apart from 'Royal Scot' none of the NBL engines were named on leaving the works. In fact the names for the other 49 were not chosen and fixed to the engines until March/April 1928. Until the names were affixed the locos ran with a steel backing for the brass nameplate fixed in position above the leading splasher.

The contract for the first 50 'Scots' was not by any stretch of imagination an overly profitable one for the NBL. The agreed price was recorded as being £7725 for each engine and tender. The cost of production of the Queens Park batch of locomotives was £189,218-12s-5d while the cost of producing the Hyde Park batch was a little higher at £196,018-1s-6d a total cost of £385,263-13s-11d. The invoice cost of 50 locomotives worked out at £386,250-0s-0d, thus showing a profit on the job of less than £1k!

Royal Scots in traffic

Deliveries were completed by NBL on 15 November 1927 and the last loco out of the works was No 6149, within only nine months of the contract being signed. All the engines were first delivered to Glasgow Polmadie Depot, from where they then went south to either Crewe or Derby, some 'Scots' of course returning to Polmadie after steam trials etc. However the first regular passenger

A rare 1930s picture of 'The Royal Scot' at speed (unknown loco). The picture was taken looking north from Sandon Bridge (before Stafford) on the WCML, with a southbound train approaching. Note the loco's narrow 'Fowler' tender dating the picture as being before 1936. The almost manicured permanent way is a joy to behold, hardly a single piece of stone out of place. Those were the days! Author's Collection

No 6100 *Royal Scot*, note the diamond-shaped 'Queens Park Works' maker's plate on the smokebox side. Author's Collection

train to be hauled by a 'Royal Scot' loco was not in England as it took place north of the border. During the third week of August 1927 locomotive No 6127 worked a return trip between Glasgow and Edinburgh. How many enthusiasts of the time were disappointed by not being aware of that low key first 'Scot' run?

Delivery from NBL to Polmadie was not in all instances a straightforward affair. Those built at Hyde Park had to have their boiler filled with cold water to above normal level in order to sit the engine well down on the springs to clear a low footbridge over the chosen route. The locos were delivered in pairs by way of a circuitous route via Kennyhill, Dalmarnock and Rutherglen to Polmadie.

In October of 1927 No 6100 was named *Royal Scot* after the train service with which it became associated. The rest of the class received an assortment of names some from long-scrapped LNWR engines and the remainder received names of a direct military/regimental origin except the last three which were named respectively *The Girl Guide, The Boy Scout* and *British Legion*. Interestingly the nameplates were all cast at either Crewe or Derby. You could easily tell which works made some of the nameplates, at least that is those with a comma in the name eg *The Artist's Rifleman*. The Derby cast plates had a comma with a square top while the Crewe castings featured a comma with a round top!

Three principal services worked by 'Royal Scots' in 1928.

Schedule Working	Mileage Run	Departure Point	Time Allowed
Euston-Kingmoor	300.8 miles	10.00 ex Euston	347 minutes
Carlisle No 12-Euston	298.2 miles	12.22 ex Carlisle	353 minutes
Glasgow-Crewe	243.3 miles	22.30 ex Glasgow	320 minutes

The original 'Scots' were by all accounts fine engines which under difficult conditions turned in some memorable performances. The 'Royal Scot' service itself was inaugurated on 26 September 1927; a scheduled London Euston-Glasgow Central service which included a non-stop run from Euston to Carlisle with a heavy 15-coach train. After the so-called 'Race to Aberdeen' the east and west route railway companies agreed to an 8¼ hour ruling between London and Glasgow.

On the Carlisle non-stops the 'Royal Scot'-hauled trains did not pull into Citadel Station and so, as far as the public were concerned, they were non-stop London-Glasgow/Edinburgh trains. The trains actually halted alongside Kingmoor sheds (down direction) and Upperby sheds (up) to change locomotives and crews.

LMSR 'Royal Scot' Class 7P 4-6-0 specification
Built: North British Locomotive Co Ltd (50 engines) Derby Works 21* (engines)
Number series: LMS 6100-6170, British Railways 46100-46170
Weight Loco: 84 tons 18 cwt (as rebuilt 83 tons 0cwt)
Weight tender: 42 tons 14cwt (as rebuilt 59 tons 11cwt)
Driving wheel: 6ft 9in diameter
Boiler pressure: 250lb/psi
Cylinders: three, 18in diameter x 26in stroke
Coal capacity: 5 tons 10 cwt (as rebuilt 9 tons 0cwt)
Water capacity: 3500 gallons (as rebuilt 4000 gallons)
Tractive effort at 85 per cent: boiler pressure 33,150lb
*Includes No 6399 *Fury* rebuilt as No (4)6170 *British Legion*

With or without smoke deflectors, which look do you prefer? No 6100 Royal Scot is seen at the Llangollen Railway 'Steel Steam & Stars Gala' on Saturday 18 April 2009, approaching Garth Y Dwr. The previously fitted smoke deflectors have been removed at the request of the owning trust. After 'rebuilding' in June1950 this locomotive would have been turned out in 'lined black' and without smoke deflectors. However the number carried would have been in the BR sequence and thus No 46100, the tender being lettered British Railways and not LMS. Smoke deflectors were later fitted to all rebuilt Royal Scot class locomotives. Author

Anglo Scots express services improved

The initial success of the first 50 Glasgow-built engines led to a further batch of 20 'Scots' being built at Derby. The order for them was placed in late 1929 and it called for them to be ready to enter traffic and be 'run in' ready for the following summer timetable. In fact the first engine left the Derby erecting shops on 23 May and was turned over to the LMS traffic department seven days later. They were given the running numbers 6150-6169 and were 'run in' from Rugby shed. The batch was built with some modifications from the NBL engines which included a necessary change in the piston valve seating arrangements.

In 1932 the 8¼ hour rule was discontinued and that meant the introduction of much improved timings for all passenger services on the LMS West Coast Main Line route, which led to a new phase of 'Royal Scot' workings. The basic details of which included the speeding up of the 'Royal Scot' train, with 35 minutes taken off the journey time, reducing the London-Glasgow timing to 7hr 40min. Also at that time the Euston-Glasgow train previously known as the '2pm corridor' was named the 'Mid Day Scot', it too being speeded up.

Records from that era showed that unpiloted a 'Scot' could take its 375-ton train up Grayrigg at 37-40mph and up Shap at speeds of 27-30mph (minimum). In the right hands these powerful locos were capable of starting a 400-ton train from a dead stop on the 1-in-75 of Shap, and still be travelling at 24-25mph as they tackled the last two miles of that formidable gradient.

The introduction of the 'Scots' on the WCML reduced the number of engine changes needed from two to one but the changing points varied, on some 'turns' being at Carlisle on others Crewe. In 1932 the class were put to work on the Crewe-Perth section of the 'Royal Highlander' sleeping-car train, a run of 292 miles. That turn included non-stop runs from Warrington to Carlisle (116.7 miles) and Carlisle to Stirling (117.7 miles). From 1934 onwards the 'Scots' were often rostered on services to Aberdeen and southbound from that city worked the 1.55pm London Fish Train.

Mileage in service (4)6100 and (4)6154

Railway statistician Doug Landau has studied the 'Engine History Cards' (LMS document CR1) of both locomotives and from information recorded on them he has been able to accurately calculate the mileages worked to the end of 1960. 'Note Engine History Cards' were kept primarily for recording repair expenditure 'per locomotive' and should not be confused with 'Locomotive Record Cards'.

Period/Loco	Mileage
1927-1932 6100 as 6100	335,021
1933-1950 6152 as 6100	1,133,164
1950-1960 Rebuild 46100	672,354
Total	2,140,539

Period/Loco	Mileage
1930-1932 6152 as 6152	156,325
1933-1945 6100 as 6152	879,036
1945-1960 Rebuild	925,324
Total	1,960,685

Therefore if you assume that the loco identity swap was never reversed the totals for each loco in its true identity would actually be slightly different ie No (4)6100 miles run 2,139,381 and (4)6152 miles run 1,961,843.

Unrebuilt 'Royal Scot' No 46134 *The Cheshire Regiment* (named *Atlas* until 1936) pictured at Dalry Road Shed Edinburgh, 28 July 1953. By April 1932 smoke deflectors had been fitted to all 70 engines of the class. Loco No 46134 was built by NBL Hyde Park Works and entered LMS service in September 1927, being withdrawn by BR in November 1962, having run in the region of 1.4 million miles in service. David Anderson

No 6399 *Fury* becomes No 6170 *British Legion*

The ill-fated high pressure loco 'Fury' was built by NBL in 1930 against works order L.858. Two other far-reaching design suggestions were made but neither came to fruition. One idea was to build a 'Scot' with Caprotti poppet-valve motion, the other being to build a compound 'Scot'.

The high pressure loco No 6399 *Fury* was built to a Schmidt super-pressure design, the loco having a triple pressure boiler. Simply explained, the firebox water tubes were under 1400 to 1800lb pressure and the distilled water within them worked within a closed circuit. The heat from that circuit generated steam at 900lb in a second circuit, which contained approximately 1½ tons of water, and the steam created therein was fed to the single high pressure inside cylinder through a piston valve.

The resultant exhaust was mixed with steam at 250lb pressure, which had been generated in the conventional fire tube part of the boiler barrel; it held approximately four tons of water. The resultant mix was then fed to the two outside low pressure cylinders.

During a trial on 10 February 1930, one of the firebox super pressure tubes burst, while the loco was at Carstairs. As a result, the Superheater Co travelling inspector was killed; the locomotive fireman and driver were seriously injured, while the LMSR inspector suffered severe shock. The engine was taken to Derby, where it lay for almost four years. Thereafter on Stanier's direct instruction it was rebuilt as a three-cylinder simple expansion taper-boiler loco and the 4-6-0 was given the number 6170 and named *British Legion*, effectively becoming the 71st member of the 'Royal Scot' class.

Which Scot went west?

It has been well documented that in 1933 loco No 6152 *The King's Dragoon Guardsman* swapped name and number with the 'first built' 6100 and went to Canada and the USA as 'Royal Scot' in order to tour and then attend the Century of Progress Exhibition in Chicago. That loco completed a tour of North America clocking up some 11,194 miles in the process, including crossing the Rocky Mountains. The two locomotives never reverted back to their old identities.

For some time after returning to the UK the loco then numbered 6100 carried a bell in commemoration of the stateside trip. No 6100 *Royal Scot* still carrying the aforementioned bell was recorded as being in Crewe Works for repair

Pictured at Crewe Works being prepared for the trip to North America the locomotive which was presented as No 6100 *Royal Scot*, but which was in all probability Derby-built sister loco No 6152 *The King's Dragoon Guardsman*. Note the smokebox-mounted train name board and the electric headlamp. The loco was also coupled to a new non-standard tender with roller bearing axleboxes for the trip 'west'. The Metcalfe Collection

during July 1934 and there is photographic evidence to that effect. David Jenkinson presents solid evidence that the identities of 6100 and 6152 were not swapped back after the Chicago trip, in his excellent publication 'The Power of the Royal Scots'.

Mr Jenkinson points out that by referring to official photographs from the time just prior to a 'Scot' loco being shipped to America it can be seen that the motion bracket behind the valve spindle (of the loco sent) is of Derby manufacture, and therefore noticeably different from the earlier North British Locomotive Co Ltd design of motion bracket carried by the original Queens Park built No 6100. Furthermore locomotive No 6152 *The King's Dragoon Guardsman* was observed in the years after the 1933 'identity swap' as carrying an NBL-style motion bracket, suggesting that loco was formerly the original No 6100.

Restored to main line running standard loco No 46115 *Scots Guardsman*. This loco was originally built for the LMS at NBL Queens Park Works in 1927 and later converted into rebuilt form in August 1947. Working approximately 1.4 million miles in service No 46115 was withdrawn by BR in January 1966. Fred Kerr

The 'Royal Scot' locomotive was shipped to North America along with a new eight-coach train of mixed type vehicles. To facilitate shipping, the engine's chassis and boiler were separated and then reassembled at the Canadian Pacific workshops in Montreal. The engine and train were shipped from London's Tilbury Docks on 11 April 1933. The Canadian Pacific Steamship 'Beaverdale' was chartered to take the 'Royal Scot' train west. The loco was stored in the hold of the vessel (in three sections) and the eight coaches were carried as deck cargo, four aft and four forward.

The first 25-day section of the 'Royal Scot' tour began on 1 May and the train reached Chicago in good time for the opening of the exhibition on 1 June.

The loco and train eventually arrived back at Tilbury aboard SS 'Beaverdale' on 5 December 1933, having completed the tour of North America during October and November of that year, eventually arriving back at the tour's Montreal starting point.

Commemorative nameplates were fitted following the 1933 trip to North America, which the preserved loco still carries. Author

It is interesting to note that the official LMS publication of the time 'The Triumph of the Royal Scot' informed our North American friends that the special train would be hauled throughout by LMS Number 6100 *Royal Scot*. Going on to state, 'it was the first of 50 locomotives of the class to be constructed in 1927 by the North British Locomotive Company of Glasgow'. Is there any need to tell them it may not have been?

Incidents in traffic, and modifications

There were two notable instances in traffic which led to 'Royal Scot Class' modifications. Firstly No 6131 *Planet* derailed at Weaver Junction (WCML) while in charge of the 'Midday Scot' on 14 January 1930. The loco came off the road as it was negotiating the junction at an estimated 70mph, a normal and not excessive speed for that section of permanent way at the time.

Following the accident inspector's findings, and subsequent recommendations, all the 'Royal Scot' bogies were modified and given stronger side springs. The modification increased the guiding effect of the bogie and also reduced wear on the leading coupled flanges. Like all 4-6-0s the 'Scots' were notorious rough riders but that aspect was noticeably improved by the enforced bogie modification.

Secondly the urgent need to fit smoke deflectors in order to combat the effects of drifting steam was highlighted by the Leighton Buzzard derailment of No

6114 *Coldstream Guardsman* in 1931. Experiments with 'smoke lifters' etc had been taking place since 1929 but when the investigation into the Leighton Buzzard incident named drifting steam (while the engine was being worked in short cut-offs) as a subsidiary cause of the derailment, the LMS realised that action needed to be taken. Large side wing plates of the type already in use by the Southern Railway were selected for use with the 'Scots', and by April 1932 the smoke deflectors had been fitted to all 70 engines of the class.

Rebuild or new build?

The Royal Scot class were rebuilt at Derby to an earlier Stanier design between 1943 and 1955. William Stanier (knighted 1943) actually ceased to work at the LMS after 1942 having taken a government post connected with wartime production, although his official resignation from the LMS did not take place until 1944. Thus the 'Scot' rebuilding programme was effectively supervised by his successors, firstly by Charles Fairburn (LMS CME 1944-45) and then by the last CME of the LMS HG Ivatt (1945-47). Ivatt stayed in post after nationalisation (in 1948) but being only then responsible for the locomotives of British Railways London Midland Region, a post he held until his retirement in 1951. He was the last of the CME's from the big four railway companies, and the position of Chief Mechanical Engineer lapsed with his retirement.

Although referred to as rebuilds the second phase 'Scots' were in reality completely new engines, with little but the cab of the original engines incorporated. Originally outshopped without smoke deflectors the rebuilt locomotives were fitted with them from 1947 onwards. The rebuilding was no doubt prompted by the fact that the life of the original boilers was coming to an end and the intensively used locos were becoming increasingly mechanically unreliable.

An increase in the number of reported incidents of 'Royal Scot' locomotive frame cracks was starting to cause the LMS some concern, the problems basically being associated with working heavier trains at higher speeds. Indeed the respected LMS locomotive engineer ES Cox highlighted the problem in a 1948 address to the Institute of Locomotive Engineers. Cox reported that the total number of frame cracks in six and seven year-old engines in 1933/4 was tolerable at only one incident in each year. However he pointed out that by 1936 the number of instances had risen to 10 and in 1942 (when the engines were 15 years old) to an alarming 37 instances.

As rebuilt the Royal Scots were not at first fitted with smoke deflectors. Loco No 46105 *Cameron Highlander* is pictured in that form on a very windy June day in 1953 at Edinburgh Princes Street about to depart with a 1.30pm service to Glasgow Central. The loco is in BR black livery with double (straw) lining and the words BRITISH RAILWAYS on the tender. This loco was rebuilt in 1948 and after running approximately 1.3 million miles in service it was withdrawn by BR on 29 December 1962. David Anderson

The rebuilding using Crewe top feed tapered LMS 2A type boilers, new cylinders, new frames (on most of the class) and incorporating very necessary mechanical modifications served to ensure that the engines would spend another 10 to 20 years in top-link service.

The Stanier taper boiler and double chimney gave the 'new' locomotives a completely different look, the later addition of 'curved to the boiler' profile 'sloping front' smoke deflectors, added to the 'new loco' look. Locomotive No 6100 was rebuilt in June 1950 having been allocated the number 46100 by British Railways.

'Above: 'A Scot on Beattock'. Loco No 46137 *The Prince of Wales' Volunteers* (South Lancashire) pictured on 17 August 1955. The original No 46137 was built at NBL Hyde Park Works in 1927 and carried the name Vesta until 1936. This loco was rebuilt in March 1955 and withdrawn by BR in November 1962 having travelled approx 1.5 million miles in service. David Anderson

Loco No 46104 *Scottish Borderer* pictured approaching Carstairs Junction station with an overnight 'sleeping car express' from London Euston in September 1958. This loco was built at NBL Queens Park Works in 1927 and rebuilt in March 1946. Having run over 1.2 million miles in service the loco was withdrawn by BR in December 1962. David Anderson

No 6100 Royal Scot, restoration

The restoration of the Bressingham 'Scot' began at Southall in 2004, and was at first expected to be completed by 2007. However in January 2009 the locomotive still needed a considerable amount of work completing in order to return it to running order. The owning trust took the decision to move the project to LNWR Heritage Crewe and the partly restored engine travelled north by low-loader on 6 February 2009.

The restoration of No 6100 was part funded by a Heritage Lottery Fund grant of £429k, approximately half the cost of the original estimated overall cost. The lottery money came with a proviso that *Royal Scot* should be up and running by a certain date. That target being missed by a big margin the LHF then set the new deadline date as the end of March 2009, that possibly being the main reason for the loco's transfer from Southall to Crewe.

The locomotive has the number 6100 stamped on various parts of the motion together with other numbers of locos from the class, including the number of identity swap loco No 6152. Once an LMS loco had been given a new identity

'The train now arrived!' Newly restored loco No 6100 undergoing a final steam test at LNWR Heritage Crewe in March 2009. Author

working practice would dictate that only the new number be adopted, to simplify component identification during subsequent visits to the works. Exceptions to that practice can of course be found, including on No 6100.

As can be expected with an engine of this age the motion and wheel sets certainly do appear to include some 'swapped' components formerly from other locomotives of the class. The number 6100 can be identified over-stamped on the number 6136 (*The Border Regiment*, a loco built by North British Locomotive Co Ltd and outshopped in September 1927, scrapped April 1964) and also over 6138 (*The London Irish Rifleman*) a loco also built by North British Locomotive Co Ltd and outshopped in September 1927, scrapped May 1963).

The left-hand 'valve spindle cross head' of No 6100 has the number 6152 (the probable identity swop loco) stamped on it, but clearly scratched across. Author

In addition the left-hand 'valve spindle cross head' (and several other valve gear parts) has the number 6152 stamped on it, but scratched across. The new number 6100 is stamped above it and as can be seen, that number has later been modified to the BR number 46100. There are other numbers which while not obviously over-stamped show the first digit (6) of the number stamped to a different depth of the next three digits (100). Evidence of a number change, ie the last three numbers ground off and the new number then stamped.

The bogie wheels/axles of the loco now under restoration are clearly marked LMS 7.1936. This is as it should be because from 1936 onwards all the 'Scots' received new unbraked and modified bogie sets. However the loco which went to America as No 6100 received a new unbraked bogie prior to the 1933 visit.

Over the years there were many opportunities for rolling chassis components to have been changed, and not least of which was during the June 1950 rebuild! The exact details of what components (if any) were changed when the loco was refurbished at Crewe in 1962/3, prior to becoming a Butlins engine, still remain a mystery?

Following the cosmetic restoration, the loco went via low-loader to Butlins Skegness holiday camp for use as a static exhibit; it was welcomed by the pipes and drums of the 1st Battalion, The Royal Scots.

In March 1971 the loco moved from the camp to the then burgeoning Bressingham Steam Museum in Norfolk, at first on loan but later being purchased outright, where it was completely overhauled and put back into working order.

The loco stayed that way until 1978; when faced with necessary and costly repairs the museum chose to take No 6100 out of service, and it once again became a static exhibit.

When originally built, the Royal Scots were paired with 3500-gallon Fowler tenders; during 1932 coal rails (greedy rails) were added to increase capacity. Many thought that the Fowler tenders spoilt the looks of an otherwise impressive-looking engine, being some 16 inches narrower than the cab.

From 1936 the Fowler tenders were replaced by vehicles of a Stanier riveted high-sided design, some from a batch originally intended for use with the Jubilee Class 4-6-0s, a number of the 'Scot' Fowler tenders going in the opposite direction to be used with the Jubilees.

For practical engineering reasons the rebuilt Scots were generally paired with a single tender for all of their working life. The tender with the restored No 6100 carries the LMS number 9338 which falls

Top: A new smokebox door inside liner is seen being fixed in place. Author

Left: Oiling 'all round' before the 6100's first 'move' in steam. Author

Every piece of the loco's motion was refurbished, tested and then refitted during the restoration of 6100. Author

within the right series of numbers and so is probably the plate from the original tender.

However the 1927 date shown on the plate would have been too early for what is now a welded tender as that construction method was only introduced by the LMS in 1936. A separate 4500 gallons capacity plate has also been attached to the vehicle following its modification, in LMS/BR use the rebuilt Scots more usually operated with 4000-gallon riveted tenders.

The current tender is undoubtedly in the style of a Stanier curved top-sides vehicle. In reality it is the amalgamation of a 'new' 5000-gallon tank, manufactured during preservation which was then mounted onto the refurbished original tender frames. The tender coupled to the other preserved Royal Scot, No 6115 *Scots Guardsman*, is of riveted construction and an original design.

Returning to the subject of 'which locomotive' it is very likely that the original locomotive number will have been stamped on the engine's frames, irrefutable evidence if found, but thus far it has not been. However the assumption that if found, the number will be 6152 (the identity swap loco) could be proved wrong, because as mentioned earlier during the rebuilding programme some frames were changed for new ones!

In which case the number stamped may be 46100? What is however without dispute is the fact that enthusiasts worldwide welcomed this loco back into steam as the legendary LMS 4-6-0 7P No 6100 *Royal Scot*.

Part of the LNWR Heritage 'Steam Team' who burned the 'midnight oil' to get the 'Royal Scot' job finished in time. Author

Richard Watkins LNWR Heritage boilershop foreman is pleased with a job well done, 19 March 2009 and 6100 has just moved in steam! Author

Welcome to Crewe. LNWR Heritage Ltd Works Manager Steve Latham with the 6100 nameplates, after the loco's arrival at Crewe for completion of its delayed return to steam. Author

Expert locomotive painter Len Crane, at work on No 6100. Author

Loco No 46121 *Highland Light Infantry, The City of Glasgow Regiment* with a Liverpool/Manchester-Glasgow on Beattock Bank, July 1959. Built 1927, rebuilt 1946, withdrawn December 1962, approx 1.5 million miles in service. David Anderson

Loco No 46133 The Green Howards (previously named *Vulcan*) on Beattock with a Carlisle-Glasgow stopping train, August 1955. Built 1927, rebuilt 1944, withdrawn February 1963, approx 1.4 million miles in service. David Anderson

Loco No 46102 *Black Watch* on the WCML near Lamington with a Glasgow-Manchester/Liverpool service, June 1958. Built 1927, rebuilt 1949, withdrawn December 1962, approx 1.3 million miles in service. David Anderson

Loco No 6100 *Royal Scot* was again fitted with smoke deflectors for the last session of the Llangollen 2009 'Steel Steam & Stars Gala'. The loco is again pictured at Garth Y Dwr, the date of this picture was Friday 24 April 2009. Author

Loco No 46107 *Argyll & Sutherland Highlander* pictured at Glasgow Polmadie MPD in June 1956. Built 1927, rebuilt 1950, withdrawn December 1962, approx 1.2 million miles in service. David Anderson

Loco No 46114 *Coldstream* Guardsman pictured at Bletchley Station in July 1963. Built 1927, rebuilt 1946, withdrawn September 1963, three months after this picture was taken. David Anderson

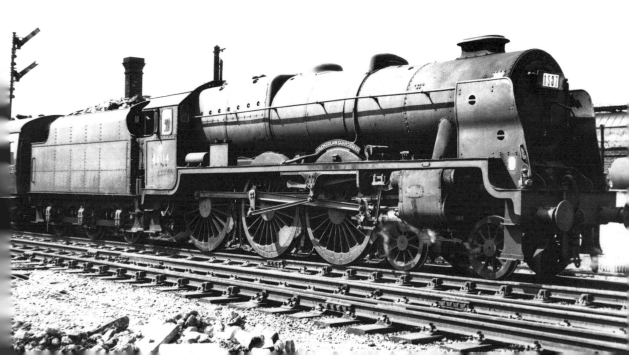

The Royal Scot 4-6-0 class (both original and rebuilt versions) are a three-cylinder locomotive design, and each cylinder can clearly be seen exhausting steam in this picture. Other LMS three-cylinder 4-6-0 steam locomotive classes were the *Patriot* class of 1930/34 and *Rebuilt Patriot* class of 1946/49, 'Jubilee' class of 1934/36 and 'Rebuilt Jubilee' class of 1942. Author

Chapter 2

BLUEBELL RAILWAY – SHOWCASE

Paul Pettitt

"I have had a passion for taking photographs for many years, but it all really started in earnest when I attended Lewes Camera Club during my late twenties. After a few weeks I felt that maybe I should join in the club activities and show off my amateurish efforts, for I was never one to shy away from ridicule and humiliation that the visiting club judges could hand out!

"Taking photographs of heritage railways began as a day out at the Bluebell Railway with my then two-year-old son, our first of two boys. On reflection I was taken aback by the fact that I had a historic time capsule just a few miles from where I live in Sussex. The Bluebell Railway satisfies many of my personal interests; I enjoy local history, the 'industrial age' and the walking in the countryside that comes with the ownership of a Bluebell lineside photographic pass.

"As I progressed with my railway photography I have become drawn into the history of local railways especially the London Brighton & South Coast Railway and Southern Railways. Even though having been born in Eastbourne (1961) I lived in Australia from 1963 to 1970, and thus missed the steam era.

"Viewing local maps it is easy to trace the routes they once took meandering though the countryside passing villages that once relied on the railway's existence to provide employment, transport and importantly fresh produce. Alas those bustling days have disappeared but fortunately they have left behind a wealth of history to enjoy, savour and photograph. I have enormous pleasure taking railway-related photographs and meeting many new friends along the way, I hope you enjoy this, a personal selection of favourite images." Paul Pettitt May 2009.

Editor's note. Those readers with an interest in photography may like to note that Paul currently uses Canon digital equipment. This selection of pictures has been taken using Canon 300D and 30D cameras and a selection of lenses which include, Canon 17-85mm EFS, Canon 70-200mm EF and Canon Compact Macro 50mm EF.

Sheffield Park Engine Shed on the Bluebell Railway, Standard 4 MT 4-6-0 No 75027
built by British Railways at Swindon in 1954 and Ivatt 2MT 2-6-2T No 41312 built by BR
at Crewe in 1952 prepare for a day in steam on ex Southern metals.

Ex LB&SCR class 'E4' 0-6-2T 2MT No 32473 (former name *Birch Grove*) running down from Three Arch Bridge to Sheffield Park. Designed by Billinton this loco was built at Brighton in 1898 and withdrawn by BR (Southern Region) in November 1962 after 64 years of almost unbroken service.

Ivatt 2MT 2-6-2T No 41312 with a demonstration goods train is pictured while 'taking the curve' on the Mid Hants Railway.

Billinton Class E4 No 32473 (*Birch Grove*) in the morning light. A really stunning study taken at Casefore Bridge on the Bluebell Railway.

Bluebell-based 'O1' class No 65 double heading with 'C' Class No 592 at sunrise on Freshfield Bank on the Bluebell Railway. The 'O1' is one of the more recent locomotives to arrive at the railway. The ex South Eastern Railway 0-6-0 No 65 was hidden from public view for over 20 years; it was restored to working order at Sheffield Park, re-entering service on 5 August 1999, the centenary of the formation of the South Eastern & Chatham Railway. The Wainwright 'C' was designed as a standard goods engine and 109 of them were built from 1900 through to 1908. They served the SECR, and in turn the SR and BR, well, 60 of the class remaining in service until 1960.

Bulleid West Country Pacific No 34028 *Eddystone* running as long-scrapped classmate No 34100 Appledore on a special Bluebell Railway Golden Arrow re-creation. Loco No 34028 *Eddystone* was built at Brighton in 1946 and rebuilt in August 1958; it was withdrawn from service by BR in May 1964.

Ex Southern Region Maunsell 'LN' class 4-6-0 No 850 Lord Nelson (*SR number*) on main line duty. This loco is also carrying a 'Golden Arrow' headboard. The loco was built at Eastleigh and outshopped in August 1926; it was withdrawn by BR in August 1962, BR number 30850.

Once more *Eddystone* in an assumed identity this time posing as 'WC' class 4-6-2 No 34021 *Dartmoor*, a loco built at Brighton in 1946, rebuilt in December 1957 and withdrawn by BR in March 1968; the loco was cut up in the August of that year. Pictured in glorious evening sunshine.

Restored Bullied unrebuilt Battle of Britain 4-6-2 No 34067 *Tangmere* crossing the river Adur near Ford, West Sussex. This loco was outshopped from Brighton in September 1947 and withdrawn by BR in November 1963.

Creation of an Autotrain working. Ex GWR Collett '14xx' class 0-4-2T No 1450 and associated driving trailer pictured rolling into Horsted Keynes Station, platform No 3. The 14xx was built at Swindon in 1935 and withdrawn by BR in May 1965.

The diminutive Terrier 'A1X' class 0-6-0T No 55 *Stepney* (BR number 32655) and Class O1 No 65 make an unusual sight as they are seen 'head on' arriving at Horsted Keynes. *Stepney* was built in 1876 at Brighton and finally withdrawn in 1960; however this loco was first withdrawn in 1925 and then returned to traffic in 1927.

Ex Somerset & Dorset Railway 7F 2-8-0 No 53809, running on the Bluebell Railway. Pictured emerging from Coneyborough Wood just as the sun begins to rise. This loco was built by Robert Stephenson & Co Ltd and entered traffic in July 1925, the engine was withdrawn by BR in March 1964.

A delightful picture of *Fenchurch* running with a rake of vintage coaching stock. The ex London Brighton & South Coast Railway A1 Stroudley Terrier 0-6-0T No 672, which was built in 1872, is the oldest locomotive based at the Bluebell Railway.

Superbly restored ex SECR 'C' class No 592 (BR number 31592) is pictured with a period observation coach on the Bluebell Railway.

Ex S&D 7F 2-8-0 No 53809 approaches New Road Bridge at Horsted Keynes Station.

A1X terrier 0-6-0T *Freshwater*, Isle of Wight loco No W8 (BR number 32646) takes the signal as it passes the down yard at Horsted Keynes. This loco also worked on the IoW system as number W2.

Horsted Keynes Station 1940s style.

The Bluebell Railway

The Bluebell Railway, which crosses the border between East and West Sussex, rejoices in the impressive claim of being the first preserved standard gauge passenger railway in the world. Opening in the spring of 1959 the venture was first known as the Lewes & East Grinstead Railway Preservation Society. The original intention of those early preservationists was to reopen a line from East Grinstead to the delightful South Downs town of Lewes. That proposal failed to gain enough local support; accordingly the newly formed railway society changed their plans and instead opted to reinstate a railway link between Sheffield Park and Horsted Keynes.

Terrier *Freshwater* waits for the goods to be loaded at Platforms 4 and 5, Horsted Keynes.

The line was famously the subject of a real headline-grabbing David and Goliath struggle, or maybe we should better say Miss Bessemer and Goliath struggle! British Railways submitted a proposal to close the line in 1954, a move hotly contested by local residents. But nevertheless the closure was approved in February 1955 and a closure date set for 28 May of that year. A battle followed between British Railways and the 'Users'; and 'The Bluebell Line' (as it had then become known) hit the national newspaper headlines as a result of the four-year-long acrimonious battle fought between the 'Users' and the transport authorities.

Shortly after the closure of the line a well-informed local resident, the redoubtable Miss Bessemer, discovered in the 1877/78 Act a clause relating to the 'Statutory Line' and immediately requested British Railways to honour their obligation. They were forced to reopen the line on 7 August 1956. The defeated British Railways subsequently took the case to the House of Commons which resulted in a public enquiry. Although severely criticised by the enquiry panel British Railways (and the Transport Commission) subsequently persuaded Parliament to repeal the special section of the aforementioned Act, as a result the line finally closed on 17 March 1958. It was later taken over by the Bluebell Railway Preservation Society.

There is a great amount of history attached to the nine-mile-long Bluebell Railway and its fascinating development and a visit to the line is highly recommended, also check out their comprehensive website. When travelling by car Sheffield Park Station is perhaps the best point to join the Bluebell Railway. The location is situated on the A275 East Grinstead-Lewes main road, about two miles north of its junction with the A272. Sheffield Park is well signposted with brown tourist direction signs from the A22 and A23 trunk roads. Horsted Keynes station is another option, and that location has plenty of parking in the field beyond the station in the summer. The station is a mile and a half north-west of the village of the same name. By rail the nearest main line station is East Grinstead which has a frequent service connecting with London Victoria. For more information see www.bluebell-railway.co.uk

Chapter 3

BEATTOCK BANK – STEAM FOCUS

David Anderson made a conscious decision to photograph as much steam action as possible between the early 1950s and 1965. Accordingly railway enthusiasts of the modern era are fortunate in being able to appreciate the power and majesty of steam as recorded by David's camera.

David's photographic style has been likened to that of the late great Eric Treacy by many appreciative observers, although the modest and unassuming son of Edinburgh would never make such a claim himself. Those enthusiasts studying his unique black and white steam era images for the first time will soon become converts to the Anderson style. Look out for 'more' as the majority of David's stunning pictures are not just about the locomotives, but also the people who worked with and around them, and indeed the whole railway scene. Each picture represents a frozen moment in 'railway' time!

Black and white photography was the only way to go when David set out on his self-imposed mission to record steam locomotives at work in many parts of the world; colour photography and processing was simply too expensive for the amateur to contemplate on a large scale. 'Large scale' was very much the plan as in the 1950s and 60s there were still a great many steam locomotives to be seen and photographically recorded. By the time that colour photography became less expensive David was already hooked on black and white, a medium he feels is ideally suited to the times of the steam locomotive.

Firstly David Anderson is an extremely knowledgeable, well travelled and well read railway enthusiast with an imaginative appreciation of all things steam, and his imagery is testament to that fact. Secondly he is a highly skilled

Ex LMS 'Jubilee' class 4-6-0 No 45731 certainly has the right name; Perseverance is pictured battling up Beattock and nearing the summit in 1958 with a Liverpool/Manchester-Glasgow express, note the horse box and fitted van. Loco No 45731 was built at Crewe in 1948 entering service in the December of that year; the loco was withdrawn by BR in October 1962.

photographer. David never set out to take steam railway pictures for you and I to appreciate, they were taken as a permanent record of something he had witnessed, appreciated and wished to keep a reminder of, and accordingly his images are all the more interesting. We are privileged to be able to share some of David Anderson's steam memories!

The northward climb of Beattock Bank on the ex Caledonian Railway (now known as the West Coast Main Line) was a firm favourite with steam enthusiasts, and David Anderson was no exception. The majority of the approximate 10-mile climb averaged out at 1-in-100 while the last punishing 1½ miles to the summit was nearer 1-in-75. The first verse from WH Auden's 'Night Mail' is particularly appropriate, even though railway travelling post offices are well and truly a thing of the past.

The Night Mail

This is the Night Mail crossing the border,
Bringing the cheque and the postal order,
Letters for the rich, letters for the poor,
The shop at the corner and the girl next door.
Pulling up Beattock, a steady climb;
The gradient's against her, but she's on time.
Past cotton-grass and moorland boulder
Shovelling white steam over her shoulder,
Snorting noisily as she passes
Silent miles of wind-bent grasses.

Stanier 'Black Five' power on Beattock Bank. Loco No 45085 is pictured near to the summit with a Carlisle-Motherwell freight in July 1960. This 5MT 4-6-0 was built by Vulcan Foundry Ltd and entered LMS service in March 1935, being withdrawn by BR in December 1962.

This Stanier 'Class 5' 4-6-0 is going well 'on the bank' with the assistance of a banking loco on the rear of the train which would have come onto the train at Beattock station. Loco No 45151 was built by Armstrong Whitworth & Co Ltd in 1935 and entered LMS service in June of that year being withdrawn by BR in December 1962. In total 842 Stanier 'Black Five' class locomotives were built between 1934 and 1951.

Ex LMS 'Jubilee' class 4-6-0 No 45640 *Frobisher* pictured at Harthope on Beattock with a London Euston-Perth express on 20 August 1955, the train has banking assistance at the rear. Loco No 45640 was built at Crewe, and entered service for the LMS in December 1934 being withdrawn by BR in March 1964. Note this locomotive is attached to a round-topped BR tender.

Ex LMS 'Jubilee' class 4-6-0 No 45697 *Achilles* pictured close to the summit with a London Euston-Perth service in August 1955. Loco No 45697 was built at Crewe for the LMS and entered service in April 1936 being withdrawn by BR in September 1967. Note in this instance that the locomotive is coupled to a 'narrower' Fowler type tender fitted with 'greedy rails', these tender were originally intended for use with the 'Royal Scot' class locomotives.

Ex LMS 'Jubilee' class 4-6-0 No 45677 *Beatty* nears the summit with a Manchester/ Liverpool-Glasgow Central service in August 1955. Loco 45677 was Crewe built by the LMS and entered service in December 1935 being withdrawn in December 1962.

Some locomotives gained a reputation with enthusiasts as being elusive, such was the case with ex LMS 'Jubilee' class 4-6-0 No 45714 *Revenge* pictured heading south with a freight on 17 August 1955. The loco was a Carlisle engine for a while and often worked evening or night turns which probably accounted for it being perceived as 'elusive'. Interestingly the Jubilee has been 'let run' by the signalman in front of a usually faster timed 'fitted freight' which is waiting in the spur (refuge siding) to the right. It may have been that the Black Five (44969) required a 'blow up' prior to continuing. In any event the engine crew faced a long reverse back, all the way to the signalbox (Beattock Summit 1015ft above sea level) in order to then move forward and gain the main line again. Loco 45714 is displaying the headlamp code for a through freight or ballast train, it being 'unfitted' the guard is probably enjoying a lively ride.

The legendary preserved ex LMS Stanier 'Princess Royal' class 4-6-2 No 46201 *Princess Elizabeth* pictured on Beattock, seen ascending with a Birmingham New Street-Glasgow Central express in summer 1958.

No 46201 pictured descending from Beattock summit near Greskine with the 'up' Mid-Day Scot in July 1959. The loco was built at Crewe by the LMS and entered service in November 1933 being withdrawn in October 1962.

Ex LMS Stanier 'Princess Coronation/Duchess' 4-6-2 No 46246 *City of Manchester* at Beattock Summit with the 'Up' Mid-Day Scot, pictured in August 1958. Loco No 46246 was built at Crewe for the LMS and entered service in August 1943, being withdrawn by BR in January 1963. Note the sloping front to the smokebox denoting a locomotive which was once streamlined (casing removed November 1948) this telltale sign later disappeared as smokeboxes were replaced.

Blasting 'up the bank' Ex LMS Stanier 'Princess Coronation/Duchess' 4-6-2 No 46225 *Duchess of Gloucester* is pictured on 9 July 1960 with a 'Down' Birmingham New Street-Glasgow Central express. This loco was also streamlined and its casing was removed in June 1948, it has also received a new smokebox. Loco No 46225 was built by the LMS at Crewe and entered service in April 1938, being withdrawn by BR in October 1964.

Ex LMS Stanier 'Princess Coronation/Duchess' 4-6-2 No 46253 *City of St. Albans* pictured near the summit with a 'Down' Royal Scot working on 9 July 1960. Loco number 46253 was built at Crewe and entered LMS service in September 1946, being withdrawn by BR in October 1964.

Ex LMS Rebuilt 'Royal Scot' 4-6-0 number 46105 *Cameron Highlander* is pictured on Beattock Bank with a 'Down' relief passenger in June 1958. This loco was built at North British Locomotive Co Ltd in 1927 and entered LMS service in August of that year. Loco 46105 was rebuilt by BR in May 1948 and withdrawn in May 1964.

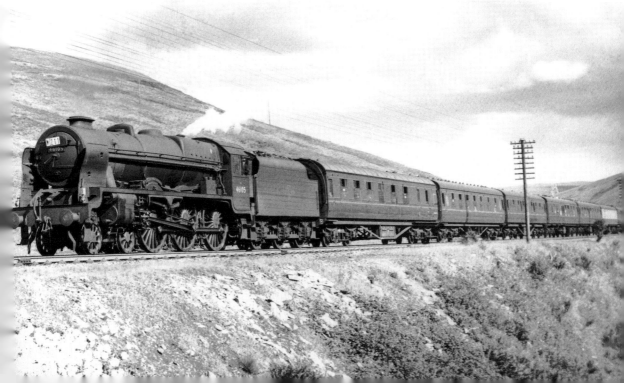

Beattock Banker! '4MT' Fairburn 4-6-4T No 42130 is pictured hard at work near Auchencastle on 19 April 1958. This loco was built at Derby for BR and entered service in December 1949, being withdrawn in December 1962.

Ex LMS Patriot 4-6-0 No 45539 *E.C.Trench* is pictured on 9 July 1960. The 1933 Crewe-built loco is descending Beattock with a Glasgow Central-Carlisle stopping train. Loco No 45539 was withdrawn from service by BR in September 1961.

Ex LMS Stanier 'Princess Royal' 4-6-2 No 46212 *Duchess of Kent* makes an impressive sight when climbing 'the bank' with a Birmingham New Street-Glasgow Central express on 15 August 1955. Loco No 46212 was built by the LMS in 1935 and entered service in October of that year being withdrawn by BR in October 1961, an impressive 26 years of mainly top-link duty.

Railway signals

This wonderful study of a steam locomotive in action also serves to highlight an interesting piece of signal equipment. To the right of the locomotive a banner repeater signal can be seen, it is of course located on the single line for the benefit of locomotive crews travelling in the opposite direction to *Nunney Castle*.

Banner repeater signals are used to provide an advanced indication of the aspect of a main signal not at that point visible to the train driver. The standard design for a banner repeater was a circular disk of translucent material with the signal arm, blunt ended for a home signal, fish-tailed for a distant, painted on in black. Mounted behind the disk is a lantern for night visibility and the disk is linked to the main signal it is employed to mimic, and so operates in concert with that signal.

A banner may be used at a location where the signal proper, and any train stopped at it, cannot be seen by the signalbox staff. The banner simply gives a prior warning in case a signal in advance of the train is set at danger. Trains were not required to stop at the banner, but only if required to do so when reaching the signal proper.

Opposite: Preserved ex GWR '4073' class Castle 4-6-0 No 5029 *Nunney Castle* pictured on 12 March 2009 at the Severn Valley Railway. Loco No 5029 was built at Swindon Works to a Collett design and entered service with the Great Western Railway in May 1934. Running some 1,523,415 miles in its working life, No 5029 was withdrawn by British Railways in December 1963. Fred Kerr

Chapter 4

THE MIGHTY PEPPERCORN A1S

At the start of 2009 arguably the most impressive preservation milestone was passed when the newly built A1 Class 4-6-2 No 60163 Tornado made its impressive first main line run. The superbly engineered machine was the first standard gauge main line steam locomotive built in the UK since British Railways Standard 9F 2-10-0 No 92220 Evening Star rolled out of Swindon Locomotive Works on 18 March 1960. Accordingly it was also the first express passenger locomotive to be built in Britain since No 71000 Duke of Gloucester left Crewe Loco Works in 1954.

Hopefully the A1 will be the first of many new UK-built main line steam locomotives, as several other 'new build' projects are currently under way. The project to build a 50th member of the long lamented Peppercorn A1 Pacific started in 1990 and creating the locomotive using 21st century steam technology has cost in the region of £3-million.

As the new loco entered its working life the 'A1 Trust' was still asking for continued monetary support. They make a very important point: "The more regular donations we receive, the quicker Tornado can pay off its debts and the more assured its working future will be." Tornado was named by Their Royal Highnesses the Prince of Wales and The Duchess of Cornwall in a ceremony held at York railway station at 10am on Thursday 19 February 2009.

Opposite: The mighty Peppercorn A1 Pacific class. Loco No 60161 North British is pictured coming off shed at Haymarket and heading down to Edinburgh Waverley Station. No 60161 was built at Doncaster and entered service with BR in December 1949. The loco was withdrawn from St Margarets MPD (64A) in October 1963 and cut up at Inverurie in March 1974. David Anderson

Design

From the very beginning the Trust regarded *Tornado* not as a replica or copy of any one of its 49 predecessors, but as the 50th AI. This simple decision gave the Trust licence to make small changes to the design to better suit modern manufacturing techniques and to fit in with the modern high speed railway, while remaining demonstrably faithful to the greater part of the original design.

Manufacturing economies

The original AI class numbered 49 locomotives, which, with many components shared with other classes, favoured manufacturing techniques suited to batch production. In particular, extensive use was made of steel castings. In most cases the cost of approval of other manufacturing techniques caused the Trust

Leaving the one-time Eastern Region at Shaftholme Junction and passing the North Eastern Railways zero mile post, No 60163 *Tornado* (but still un-named at that time) gets into its stride at Joan Croft Junction on 1 February 2009. Note the plain (un-lipped) chimney. Brian Sharpe

to choose steel castings as per the originals. However for some items such as the star stay which supports the brake cylinder, a fabrication was produced. Extensive use has been made of patterns fashioned from expanded polystyrene which are ideal for one-off items, and cost between one third and a half of a comparable wood pattern.

The principal change from the original design concerns the boiler. *Tornado's* boiler was designed as a fully welded vessel with a steel firebox as opposed to the original A1 design that was riveted and had a copper firebox. The reason is that, with the exception of a small cottage industry which supports the existing preservation movement, there is no capacity to produce a large riveted boiler in the modern pressure vessel industry.

This method of construction did not significantly increase the technical risk as extensive use was made of welded boilers and steel fireboxes in the USA, and other overseas countries. In the UK the successful Bulleid designed Merchant Navy and West Country classes had fully welded inner and outer fireboxes made from steel.

Requirements for modern operating conditions

• **Brakes**: the A1 class was equipped with a steam brake for the locomotive and vacuum brake for the train. As it is expected that the locomotive will spend most of its operating time on the main line, the Trust has decided to make air brakes the primary braking system for the locomotive. To enable the locomotive to haul vacuum-braked stock on heritage railways, a vacuum ejector is fitted with the vacuum train pipe being controlled through an air/vacuum proportional valve. In addition to the automatic fail-safe air brake system, the locomotive is being equipped with a straight air brake to assist with shunting and coupling.

• **AWS/TPWS**: the original locomotives were fitted with the BR vacuum brake AWS (Automatic Warning System). In modern main line service *Tornado* will require the new TPWS (Train Protection and Warning System). This is designed to be a direct replacement for the AWS as fitted to air braked diesel and electric stock; however it is not so readily swapped with the vacuum AWS equipment. Modern operating conditions require a data recorder to be fitted on all motive power running on Network Rail. Radio will also be fitted on *Tornado*.

• **Electrical system**: arising from the above plus the possible later fitment of

New build Peppercorn 'A1' 4-6-2 locomotive No 60163 pictured 'in primer' during running in trials at the Great Central Railway in 2008. Note the lipped chimney. Brian Sharpe

video cameras to relay locomotive action to the train, there will be a significantly increased requirement for electrical power on the locomotive. As built, the A1s had a 350W 24v AC turbo alternator fitted which powered light bulbs for marker lights, cab gauge lighting and certain lights for maintenance purposes. When the AWS was fitted, a separate 24v battery set was provided.

- *Tornado* **therefore has a dual battery system**: a vital service battery to power the AWS/TPWS and cab radio and a general services battery for the other demands. The alternators continuously charge these, backed up if necessary by an auxiliary generator in the support coach or a mains shore supply when stabled. The charging circuitry has been designed to ensure preferential charging of the vital services battery.

Range and capacity

Tornado's tender has been redesigned internally eliminating the water scoop and increasing the water capacity from 5000 gallons (22,700 litres) to around 6200 gallons (28,150 litres) and reducing coal capacity from nine tons to 7.5 tons.

The range of a steam locomotive is governed by water capacity, lubricant consumption and fuel capacity. Water is the most significant limitation with most locomotives hauling loaded trains at express speeds being limited to about 100 miles (160 km) between fillings of the tender. For the A1 class an average of 40-45 gallons (113-137 litres) per mile is to be expected. Thus the standard 5000 gallons (22,700 litres) capacity of the tender allowed an average of about 100 miles (160 km) allowing 500 gallons (2270 litres) in reserve.

With the capacity of the *Tornado* tender augmented to 6200 gallons (27,240 litres) plus a possible 8000 gallons (36,320 litres) in a future second vehicle, a range of around 300 miles (480 km) non-stop would be practicable. This would allow operation from Euston to Carlisle or King's Cross to Newcastle.

Royal Train duty. The newly named 50th A1 No 60163 *Tornado* is pictured at Burton Salmon on 19 February 2009. Note the three-lamp 'Royal Train' code, only a train carrying the reigning monarch is authorised to carry the full four-lamp code. Jeff Colledge

The Angel of the North; *Tornado* **arrives at Tyne Yard for servicing on 31 January 2009.**
Brian Sharpe

Full oil pots and lubricators would ensure a comfortable 300-mile (480km) range – the 'Elizabethan' non-stop runs totalled about 400 miles (640km) with the shed runs at either end. The original locomotives had a coal capacity of nine tons of coal which gave about 350 miles (560km) of range. *Tornado's* reduced coal capacity of 7.5 tons will give a range of about 290 miles (470km).

The A1 class was designed to cope with the heaviest regular East Coast trains of the post-war period. These were regularly loaded to 15 coaches or 550 tons. The locomotives were capable of maintaining 60-70 miles per hour (95-110km/hr) on level track. However, the asset of *Tornado* will be the ability to haul lighter (10-11 coach trains) at higher speeds to fit in with modern traffic patterns.

The Original A1s

The LNER A1s were designed by Arthur H Peppercorn, the last Chief Mechanical Engineer of the London & North Eastern Railway. They were the last in a line of famous express passenger steam locomotives for the East Coast

Main Line, an auspicious list which included the Stirling Singles, the Ivatt Atlantics and the Gresley Pacifics.

Edward Thompson introduced a prototype locomotive in 1945 which was later classified A1/1 and ran with BR number 60113; it was named *Great Northern*. The Thompson prototype was a rebuild of Gresley's Doncaster-built prototype pacific No 4470, also named *Great Northern*, and first introduced in 1922. That locomotive was withdrawn on 19 November 1962 and cut up by British Railways at Doncaster Works in May 1963.

The original 49 Peppercorn Class A1s were ordered by the LNER and built at Doncaster (26 locos) and Darlington (23 locos) for British Railways (BR) in 1948/9, immediately after the nationalisation of the railways. As designed they were 6ft 8in versions of the Class A2 Pacific and were ideally suited for the post-war railway world of poor maintenance and heavy trains. Equipped with a huge 50sq ft grate, the locos were able to use lower grade coal than their predecessors. The locos at first ran without names, but eventually they all carried names on the side of their smoke deflectors.

Class A1 4-6-2 No 60152 *Holyrood* eases off Haymarket Shed at Haymarket Central Junction on 8 September 1957. Edinburgh to Glasgow lines in the foreground with the depot access tracks to the left. Former Caledonian Railway Edinburgh (Princes Street) to Granton and Leith lines run across the main lines, all now removed. Loco No 60152 entered traffic on 8 July 1949 and was built at Darlington Works, first shed under BR Haymarket (64B) one of five so allocated. Withdrawn from York North (50A) the loco was cut up at Cashmore's, Great Bridge, on 31 August 1965. David Anderson

Another Scottish-based A1 Pacific No 60162 *Saint Johnstoun* is pictured passing Haymarket Shed with an Edinburgh Waverley-Aberdeen express in the summer of 1956. Loco No 60162 entered traffic for BR on 23 December 1949 and was built at Doncaster Works, first shed under BR Haymarket (64B) one of five so allocated. Withdrawn 28 October 1963 from St Margarets (64A) the loco was cut up 28 February 1964 Inverurie Works (BR) David Anderson

The final five A1s were equipped with roller bearings enabling them to be in service for an average of 118,000 miles between heavy repairs, making the A1s the cheapest to run of all British steam locomotives in the same category. They were also among the most reliable of all of the express passenger steam locomotives owned by British Railways.

Unfortunately, the rapid onset of dieselisation in the 1960s meant that all were scrapped, after an average life in traffic of only 15 years. There was an attempt to save the last, 60145 *Saint Mungo*; but this unfortunately failed and it too was withdrawn in June 1966 and scrapped in September of the same year, therefore no members of the class passed into preservation. In 2009 that wrong was well and truly righted by the A1 Trust.

The publishers are indebted to the A1 Trust for permission to reproduce 60163 'design and build' technical information.

For more information about 60163 *Tornado* please visit www.a1steam.com

LNER/BR A1 Class Information

Designed by AH Peppercorn. Introduced 1948–49

Built by LNER/BR, Darlington and Doncaster Works

Total number built: 49

British Railways number series 60114-60162 (1948 onwards)

Loco specification:

Tractive effort: 29,835lb at 85 per cent boiler pressure

Weight: Loco 104 tons 2cwt

Tender: 60 tons 7cwt

Driving wheel: 6ft 8in

Boiler press: 250lb/sq in Superheated.

Cylinders: Three 19in x 26in

Valve gear: Walschaerts (piston valves)

Coal capacity: 8 tons (*Tornado* 7.5 tons)

Water capacity: 5000 gallons (*Tornado* 6200 gallons)

On Royal Train duty after the February 2009 'Royal' naming ceremony A1 Tornado at speed near Colton. HRH Prince of Wales Prince Charles in the driving seat! Fred Kerr

No 60115 'Meg Merrilies' Class A1. Proud engine crew at Wakefield (56A) in September 1961. Entered into traffic 3 September 1948, built Doncaster Works. Withdrawn 12 November 1962 from Leeds Copley Hill (37B), cut 24 May 1963 at Doncaster Works. First shed under BR Gateshead (52A) as one of 12 allocated A1 locos. Author's Collection

Loco No 60114 *W.P.Allen* Class A1. Pictured coming off the coaling plant at York (50A) in October 1964. Entered into traffic 6 August 1948, built Doncaster Works. Withdrawn 26 December 1964 from 36A Doncaster, cut 28 February 1965 at Hughes Bolckows, North Blyth. First shed under BR King's Cross (34A) as one of nine allocated locos A1/1 and A1 locos. Author's Collection

No 60113 *Great Northern* classified A1/1, which was Thompson's prototype loco. Pictured at York in 1959. Entered into traffic April 1922 from LNER Doncaster Works as LNER No 4470 then 113, rebuilt 1945, numbered 60113 in 1948. Withdrawn 19 November 1962 from Doncaster (36A) cut up 28 February 1963 at BR Doncaster Works. First shed under BR Kings Cross (34A) as one of nine locos allocated ie one A1/1 and eight A1 locos. Author's Collection

No 60138 *Boswell* Class A1, pictured at York in April 1964, Entered into traffic 10 December 1948, built BR Darlington Works. Withdrawn 4 October 1965 from York North (50A) cut up 30 November 1965 at Ward's, Killamarsh. First shed under BR York North as one of six allocated A1 locos. Author's Collection

No 60147 *North Eastern* Class A1, pictured at York in 1963. Entered into traffic 13 April 1949 built BR Darlington Works. Withdrawn 28 August 1964 from York North (50A) cut up 30 November 1964 at Drapers, Hull. First shed under BR Gateshead (52A) as one of 12 allocated A1 locos. Author's Collection

No 60120 *Kittiwake* Class A1 pictured on *Yorkshire Pullman* duty at Doncaster 1955. Entered into traffic 10 December 1948, built BR Doncaster Works. Withdrawn 20 January 1964 from York North (50A) cut up 28 January 1964 at BR Darlington Works. First shed under BR Kings Cross (34A) as one of nine locos allocated ie one A1/1 and eight A1 locos. The 350W 24v AC turbo alternator can clearly be seen located inside the offside smoke deflector. Author's Collection

No 60157 *Great Eastern* Class A1, pictured on *Flying Scotsman* duty at Doncaster in 1958. Entered into traffic 3 November 1949, built BR Doncaster Works. Withdrawn 10 January 1965 cut up 28 February 1965 at Drapers, Hull. First shed under BR Kings Cross (34A) as one of nine locos allocated ie one A1/1 and eight A1 loccs. Author's Collection

No 60151 *Midlothian* Class A1 pictured outside Doncaster Works in 1963. Entered into traffic 30 June 1949, built BR Darlington Works. Withdrawn 24 November 1965 from York North (50A) and cut up 31 January 1966 at George W Station Steel, Wath-upon-Dearne. First shed under BR Gateshead (52A) as one of 12 allocated A1 locos. Author's Collection

Loco No 60125 *Scottish Union* Class A1. Entered into traffic 22 April 1949, built Doncaster Works. Withdrawn 4 July 1964 from Doncaster (36A) cut up 31 August 1964 at Cox & Danks, Wadsley Bridge. Author's Collection

Loco No 60157 *Great Eastern* Class A1, on *Aberdonian* duty. Entered into traffic 3 November 1949, built BR Doncaster Works. Withdrawn 10 January 1965 cut up 28 February 1965 at Drapers, Hull. First shed under BR King's Cross (34A) Author's Collection

The AI Class were originally fitted with plain-topped chimneys but those were later replaced with chimneys formed with a lipped top, a move which many said greatly improved the appearance of the engines, judge for yourself! *Tornado* entered main line service with a plain chimney to keep faith with the apple green livery which has been initially applied. However the loco completed its 2008 test runs with a 'lipped version' and its chimney will revert to that style when the first livery change is made, possibly in 2010/11.

Loco No 60120 *Kittiwake* pictured in full cry during 1963, again with a lipped chimney.
Author's Collection

Loco No 60129 *Guy Mannering* seen in the 1950s at Wrenthorpe, still sporting an original-style plain chimney. Author's Collection

Loco No 60125 *Scottish Union* seen at Doncaster in 1962 with lipped chimney. Author's Collection

What's in a Name?

The A1 Class carried what many consider to be the most eclectic set of names of any steam locomotive class. There were seven different categories in all, the largest group being 13 names of racehorses. There were six named after birds (four of them having been originally attached to A4 Class locomotives. The names of six locomotive engineers were celebrated as were four railway companies, with a fifth railway company name allocated to the A1/1 prototype. Ten A1s were named in deference to the life and works of Sir Walter Scott while a further batch of nine were named after royal residences, cities and areas of Scotland, all of those 19 Scottish names were originally carried on North British Railway locomotives.

Number	Name	Origin of Name
60113*	GREAT NORTHERN	The Great Northern Railway
60114	W. P. ALLEN	LNER locomotive driver who became a member of the Railway Executive in 1948
60115	MEG MERRILIES	A character in Guy Mannering, Sir Walter Scott novel
60116	HAL O'THE WYND	A character in The Fair Maid of Perth, Sir Walter Scott novel
60117	BOIS ROUSSEL	1938 Derby winner
60118	ARCHIBALD STURROCK	Locomotive Superintendent, Great Northern Railway 1850/66
60119	PATRICK STIRLING	Locomotive Superintendent, Great Northern Railway 1866/95
60120	KITTIWAKE	A medium-sized gull
60121	SILURIAN	1923 Doncaster Cup winner
60122	CURLEW	Large wading bird with a long curved bill
60123	H. A. IVATT	Locomotive Superintendent, GNR. 1895/1911
60124	KENILWORTH	A Sir Walter Scott novel
60125	SCOTTISH UNION	1938 St Leger winner
60126	SIR VINCENT RAVEN	Chief Mechanical Engineer North Eastern Railway 1910/22
60127	WILSON WORSDELL	Loco Superintendant/ CME of NER 1890 to 1910
60128	BONGRACE	1926 Doncaster Cup winner
60129	GUY MANNERING	A Sir Walter Scott novel
60130	KESTREL	Common British bird of prey
60131	OSPREY	Large fish-eating bird of prey
60132	MARMION	A narrative poem by Sir Walter Scott
60133	POMMERN	Legendary racehorse, English triple crown winner
60134	FOXHUNTER	1932 Doncaster Cup winner
60135	MADGE WILDFIRE	A character in Sir Walter Scott's novel Heart of Midlothian
60136	ALCAZAR	1934 Doncaster Cup winner
60137	REDGAUNTLET	A Sir Walter Scott novel
60138	BOSWELL	1936 St Leger winner
60139	SEA EAGLE	Rare British white-tailed eagle
60140	BALMORAL	Highland royal retreat
60141	ABBOTSFORD	Home of Sir Walter Scott from 1811 until his death
60142	EDWARD FLETCHER	Loco Superintendent NER 1845 to 1883
60143	SIR WALTER SCOTT	The man himself, 1771 to 1832
60144	KING'S COURIER	1900 Doncaster Cup winner
60145	SAINT MUNGO	The founder of Glasgow, aka Saint Kentigern, 518 to 603
60146	PEREGRINE	The largest resident British falcon
60147	NORTH EASTERN	North Eastern Railway
60148*	ABOYEUR	1913 Derby winner, after first horse past the post disqualified
60149	AMADIS	1909 Doncaster Cup winner
60150	WILLBROOK	1914 Doncaster Cup winner
60151	MIDLOTHIAN	Scottish county
60152	HOLYROOD	Monarch's official residence in Edinburgh
60153	FLAMBOYANT	1921 Doncaster Cup winner
60154	BON ACCORD	The motto on the arms of the city of Aberdeen
60155	BORDERER	A person from the Scottish borders
60156	GREAT CENTRAL	Great Central Railway
60157	GREAT EASTERN	Great Eastern Railway
60158	ABERDONIAN	A native of Aberdeen
60159	BONNIE DUNDEE	A character from a Sir Walter Scott song
60160	AULD REEKIE	Slang (nick name) for Edinburgh referring to its once smoky atmosphere
60161	NORTH BRITISH	North British Railway
60162b	SAINT JOHNSTOUN	Perth's former name

*Class A1/1 prototype locomotive.

Chapter 5

CHURNET VALLEY – SHOWCASE

David Gibson

"My interest in photography was nurtured by my father. He used to develop his own black and white photographs in a makeshift darkroom at our home and I used to watch fascinated as the pictures gradually appeared, to my young eyes as if by magic! I was from that time hooked on photography at least that is the taking of images, and not necessarily the thought of spending long hours in a darkened room.

"At first I used a second-hand 120 camera I had saved up to buy, I think that the cost of actually paying to get my pictures processed helped to make me a better photographer, I was careful not to waste film etc. On the equipment front things got better when my father gave me his old 35mm camera. Another mystery of the 'art' came with it, a Weston II light meter. I used that ancient meter for years until I found it too difficult to read the small figures, it is still one of my treasured possessions.

"The first 'real' camera I bought was an Olympus OMI, state of the art at the time. I got it at the right price as my brother-in-law had brought it home with him from Hong Kong, where he had been stationed. After a couple of years I bought another camera, this time again an Olympus, a more modern OM2n model. I gathered a good selection of matching lenses over the years to support the Olympus system. At this point most of my photographs were of family, holidays and local scenes.

"Then about ten years ago everything changed, I discovered the Churnet Valley Railway. The railway and heritage centre was just becoming established

The way it used to be. Loco number 44422 is one of three survivors from a class of 4F 0-6-0 locomotives originally designed by Fowler as a standard Midland Railway freight engine. This recreation at Kingsley & Froghall station is a faithful one, as the LMS and later BR used this freight type extensively on passenger work. This particular locomotive was built at Derby Works in 1927 and entered traffic with the LMS in October of that year, being withdrawn in June 1965.

and the visits there awoke another of my boyhood passions, steam engines! The railway developed steadily and so there was always something new to put a lens on. At about the same time I made a change from film and transparency to digital. Lower processing cost, that is of course apart from a computer system of the right specification.

"After much soul searching I chose a basic Canon digital camera, liked the results and eventually moved on to a Canon DSI MkII which, with the right selection of lenses, I find perfect for railway photography. I am a registered volunteer at the CVR and over the past couple of years I have started to assemble a photographic archive for them.

"Railway photography now takes me all over the country, and indeed often to other parts of the world. In doing so I have had a good deal of my work published and also made a great many friends. I hope you enjoy this personal selection from some of my favourite CVR images." **David Gibson May 2009**.

A string of locomotives head through Consall Forge station; leading the way is ex LMS 'Jinty' 0-6-0 No 47279 a loco built by Vulcan Foundry Ltd in 1924 and withdrawn by BR in December 1966. In the middle is ex LMS 'Black Five' 4-6-0 No 45231 built by Armstrong Whitworth Co Ltd in 1936 and withdrawn by BR at the end of steam working in August 1968. Bringing up the rear is an American-built 'S160' 2-8-0 No 5197. The S160 is one of two at the CVR, sister loco No 6064 was still under restoration in 2009.

The Churnet Valley Railway has often been referred to as 'Little Switzerland' and so appropriately David has included some winter pictures. A December scene in the shed yard at Cheddleton. Locos on view No 44422, No 45231 (The Sherwood Forester name was bestowed after preservation) and S160 No 5197.

Visiting 'Black Five' 4-6-0 No 45231 hurries away from Kingsley & Froghall station with a service to Cheddleton. This loco is one of 327 of the class built by Armstrong Whitworth Co Ltd, an order which was at the time the biggest single loco order ever placed by a railway company. Black Five class locos were also built by Vulcan Foundry (100) Derby Works (100) Horwich Works (105) and Crewe Works (210) between 1934 and 1951.

Smartly turned out ex GWR 2-6-2T No 5199 shines in the bright sunshine with a Cambrian Coast Express re-creation, as the winter snow starts to melt. There are 10 examples of the '5101' class in preservation and in January 2009 four examples were operational. Loco No 5199 was built at Swindon Works in 1935 and withdrawn by BR in 1963.

Visiting 1954 Brighton-built BR Standard 'Class 4 Tank' No 80098 is pictured making a spirited start from Cheddleton with the railway's S160 coupled inside (tender to tender). This loco is one of 15 of the class preserved; in January 2009 six of those were reported as being operational.

Wildlife artist and pioneer railway preservationist David Shepherd is pictured on the footplate of his ex BR Standard 9F 2-10-0 freight locomotive No 92203 during a visit to the CVR. In preservation this impressive loco carries the name *Black Prince*. Built at Swindon in 1959 No 92203 is one of nine preserved Standard 9F locomotives; in January 2009 three of those were reported as being operational.

National Collection Locomotive ex LNWR/LMS 'G2 Super D' 7F 0-8-0 No 49395 pictured during a visit to the railway. Built at Crewe in 1921 this loco was withdrawn from service by BR in 1959. This iconic freight locomotive was restored for the NRM by London & North Western Railway Heritage Co Ltd at their Crewe works which is only a stone's throw from where it was built.

The ex GWR speed record-breaking 4-4-0 No 3440 City of Truro, which since restoration has regularly visited preserved railways. Loco No 3440 is pictured on the run-round loop at Kingley & Froghall station. The 1903 Swindon-built Churchward engine is credited with being the first steam locomotive to exceed 100mph and is also the 2000th loco built at Swindon Works. On 9 May 1904 *City of Truro* achieved a speed of 102.3mph on the descent of Wellington Bank.

In 1912 this loco was renumbered 3717 and after almost 20 years in top link service the 4-4-0 was withdrawn, and in 1931 placed on display in York Museum. But the iconic loco was not destined to remain a static exhibit, in 1957 No 3717 was taken out of the museum and sent to Swindon Works for a complete overhaul pending a return to steam. For the following four years, and by that time renumbered 3440, the engine appeared around the network hauling enthusiast specials. In 1961 *City of Truro* returned to the National Railway Museum for a further period of static display. However No 3440 was returned to steam again in February 2004 the centenary year of the record-breaking run, following a £130,000 refit. In January 2009 the GWR centenarian was still steaming!

City of Truro on 'Moorlander' dining train duty at the CVR is pictured departing from Consall Forge station with a train for Kingsley & Froghall.

Trains crossing at Consall Forge station. The railway is between the river Caldon and the Caldon Canal within the picturesque Churnet Valley, in this view the canal is to the right and the river to the left as is the station car park. Loco number 44422 ex LMS 4F 0-6-0 is seen departing with a train for Kingsley & Froghall.

The still of the night. Ex LMS 'Jinty' 0-6-0 No 47279 seen in Cheddleton shed yard. The 'Jinty' is one of 10 examples of that popular class which have been saved by preservationists; in January 2009 four of those were reported as being operational. Between 1924 and 1931 a total of 415 '3F' 0-6-0 'Jinty' types were built for the LMS and a further seven for the Somerset & Dorset Joint Railway.

A recreated scene from the 1960s, 'change over years'. Standard tank No 80098 with a train of vans is seen in Cheddleton Station with an 'incomer', a Diesel Mechanical Unit (DMU). Like many preserved railways the CVR holds special photographic charter events and this memory-provoking image was captured during one such occasion.

An evocative image of ex LNER 'K1' 2-6-0 No 61994 *The Great Marquess*, seen departing from Consall Forge, a magical mix of steam smoke and mist. Loco No 61994 was built at Darlington Works for the LNER and entered service in July 1938, being withdrawn by BR in December 1961.

Restored ex industrial locomotives have long been the mainstays of motive power for many preserved railways, indeed smaller engines often outnumber the 'big engines' in regular use. This 0-6-0 Saddle Tank numbered 68030 was never a BR locomotive, it was rescued from industrial use, and has been numbered as a sister loco which once worked the famous Cromford & High Peak line for British Railways.

Ex GWR Pannier Tank 0-6-0 No 5764 seen during a visit to the CVR. Collett-designed '57xx' pannier tanks were built for the GWR between 1929 and 1939 and thankfully 17 of them have survived into preservation, they are ideal locomotives for use on preserved railways. In January 2009 there were nine of the class reported as being operational. Loco No 5764 was once operated by London Underground as No L95 it was sold to LT in 1960 and retired by them in 1971, thus outlasting steam on BR.

American-built 'S160' 2-8-0 No 5197 seen running alongside the Caldon Canal. These 2-8-0 locomotives were built by American Locomotive Company (ALCO), Baldwin Locomotive Company and Lima Locomotive Company for the United States Army Transportation Corps of Engineers (USATE). Loco No 5197 was built as works No 8856 in 1945 and was shipped directly from the US to China in 1945 and hauled coal trains there until the mid 1990s, as Chinese State Railway's class KD6 No 463. The loco was then rescued from being scrapped by the Chinese coal industry, brought to the UK and restored at the Llangollen Railway, entering service there in 1999. The 'S160' moved to the CVR in February in 2001. Another of the class, USATC number 6046, was reported as being under restoration at the railway in 2009.

Visiting loco Bulleid 'Rebuilt Merchant Navy' class Pacific. No 35005 *Canadian Pacific* is pictured leaving Consall Forge station; S160 No 5157 is waiting in the other platform with a demonstration freight train. Loco No 35005 was built at Eastleigh and entered service for the Southern Railway in January 1942, it was rebuilt by BR in 1959 and withdrawn by them in October 1965.

The Churnet Valley Railway

The last sand train ran from Oakamoor in 1988, and nearly four years later British Railways declared the line non-operational. In late 1992 an application was made for a Light Railway Order to the Secretary of State for Transport by the Churnet Valley Railway (1992) plc. A £7000 feasibility study, jointly funded by the Staffordshire County Council, Staffordshire Moorlands District Council and volunteers in 1989, had shown that tremendous tourist potential existed if the seven miles of track through beautiful scenery from Leekbrook Junction to Oakamoor Quarry was to be reopened.

The line was subsequently purchased at a cost of £250,000 and services commenced over the first mile of line between Cheddleton station and Leekbrook Junction during August Bank holiday 1996. The railway subsequently expanded first to Consall in 1998 and then Kingsley & Froghall in August 2001, where a new period-style station was built.

With the future of an expansion to the town of Leek in prospect and a reopening of the Caldon Low branch towards Waterhouses, the terminus with the long lamented Leek & Manifold Railway, now looking likely since a company associated with the CVR has gained a lease on the line, it looks like busy and exciting times lie ahead for the CVR

Cheddleton station, home of the Churnet Valley Railway is situated three miles south of the textile market town of Leek in Staffordshire. The whole site is seen as a 'living museum' preserving part of Britain's heritage, with the Cheddleton buildings being restored to represent a typical country station of the original operating company the North Staffordshire Railway (Knotty).

Consall Forge features working signalling of the passing loop and a 'rare' waiting shelter of Midland Railway design, which overhangs the canal. Of course, the highlight of any visit is the sight and smell of a steam locomotive, which you can now travel behind over $5\frac{1}{4}$ miles of the CVR line on most weekends and weekdays during summer.

The Churnet valley is renowned for its natural beauty, being honeycombed with pleasant walkways where visitors can readily sample the superb scenery and many places of interest. Within a short radius of all the station sites is the picturesque river Churnet and Caldon Canal.

The CVR is open Saturdays and Sundays from March to October. A DMU service usually operates on Saturdays. Wednesdays, Fridays and weekends are steam hauled during the summer months and Tuesday and Thursdays are diesel

Five locomotives in steam, Cheddleton shed yard prior to a 2008 Steam Gala event. Left to right ex LNER 'V2' No 4471 *Green Arrow*, ex USATC 'S160' No 5197, ex BR 'Standard 4' Tank No 80098, ex LNWR/LMS 'Super D' No 49395 and ex LMS Fowler '4F' No 44422.

services. Outside these times, footplate experiences, school parties, 'Moorlander Limited' Wine & Dine evenings and charter services are all operated on a regular basis.

The station is open most days from 10.30am to 6pm. For special events, prior booking is essential. Enquiries from schools are especially welcome. For more details, contact Cheddleton Station on 01538 360522 or see www.churnet-valley-railway.co.uk

Chapter 6

OXFORD – STEAM FOCUS

Of the many popular locations around the network which attracted the attention of railway enthusiasts during the British Railways 'steam era', Oxford was among the most interesting. Locomotives originating from all four of the post-grouping companies, and many of later BR origin could regularly be observed at work, being serviced or simply resting between turns.

The closure of the long lamented Somerset & Dorset Railway in 1962 meant that the famous 'Pines Express' (Manchester-Bournemouth service) was diverted to run via Oxford a move which, much to the delight of local enthusiasts, regularly brought Bulleid Pacific locomotives to the area.

Of course the main focus at Oxford during that period were ex Great Western locomotives of which the railway had its own varied allocation, the BR Western Region motive power depot at Oxford was listed as 81F, a code it shared with sub sheds at Abingdon and Fairford. Almost every ex GWR locomotive type could be seen regularly at Oxford and the famous GWR 'Cathedrals Express' called at the station. An earlier LNWR depot and station to the north of the present station called Rewley Road closed in 1951 and the unique structure has been removed and rebuilt at the Buckinghamshire Railway Centre, Quainton Road near Aylesbury.

Long known and admired for its 'dreaming spires' the city's famous university has an interesting connection with 'the railway enthusiast'. The Oxford Railway Club was formed in 1932; it soon attracted notoriety but not exactly for its members' appreciation of all things 'railway', more for their exuberant excesses.

Founder members included the writer Evelyn Waugh (1903-1966) an English novelist and satirist whose name was in modern times brought to the attention of millions following the TV dramatisation of his classic work Brideshead Revisited. Another prominent member was Harold Acton (1904-1994) a writer and scholar who listed as his principal recreation 'hunting the philistines'. From the balcony of his Oxford rooms he famously declaimed passages from 'The Waste Land', through a megaphone.

The aim of the mainly extrovert society members was to consume vast quantities food and drink while travelling by rail; thankfully for other travellers the group usually held their high-spirited gastronomic gatherings in specially reserved dining cars. After one such excursion reportedly got out of control the university proctors saw fit to close the club down for a time. But it was soon resurrected and the members carried on holding their railway dining car binges up until 1939. This club is not to be confused with the perfectly respectable Oxford University Railway Society.

Ex GWR Collett '4073' Castle class 4-6-0 locomotive No 7001 *Sir James Milne*. This locomotive was named *Denbigh Castle* when first allocated to traffic in May 1946 but was renamed in February 1948. The name *Denbigh Castle* was later allocated to another of the class No 7032 built in 1950. Swindon-built Loco No 7001 was withdrawn by British Railways in September 1963 having run 838,604 miles in service. Pictured in the shed yard at Oxford in May 1961.

Each of David Anderson's wonderful 'Oxford' images tell a railway story all of their own, with not just the locomotives catching the eye. Look out for the fascinating selection of signals, railway personnel, station notices and track layouts etc. We have even included an image showing a Diesel Multiple Unit simply because it is faithful to those changing times and can be seen in stark contrast with one of the locomotive types it was designed to replace.

On the last day of passenger services on the Oxford-Fairford branch, 16 June 1962, '57xx' class 0-6-0PT No 9654 waits at Oxford station northern bay platform. To mark the occasion the ex GWR pannier tank carries an 'Oxford University Railway Society' headboard. The tank locomotive was built at Swindon in 1946 and withdrawn by BR in October 1964. The DMU standing alongside is waiting to work to Kingham.

Swindon-built ex GWR Collett '4073' Castle class 4-6-0 locomotive No 7004 *Eastnor Castle* is pictured leaving Oxford on a 2.15pm service to London Paddington. Loco Swindon built No 7004 entered traffic in June 1946 and was withdrawn by BR in January 1964 having run some 876,349 miles in service.

Swindon-built 7027 ex GWR Collett '4073' Castle class 4-6-0 locomotive No 7027 *Thornbury Castle* leaving Oxford with a Worcester/Hereford-Paddington train in 1962. Locomotive No 7027 was outshopped in August 1949 and withdrawn by BR in December 1963. This example of the class is preserved awaiting restoration.

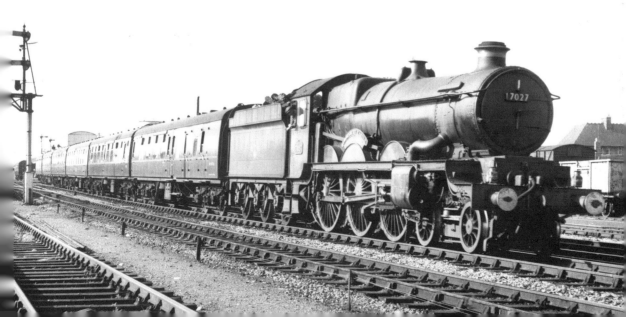

Swindon-built ex GWR Collett '4073' Castle class 4-6-0 locomotive No 7006 *Lydford Castle* is preparing to depart the north end of Oxford station with the 2.07pm service to Banbury. Built in June 1946 this loco was withdrawn in December 1963 having run some 789,052 miles in service, mostly for BR. The metal signal gantry was erected in 1959 to replace earlier GWR signals. Note the timber-built GWR loco shed to the left. To the front right of the engine can be seen part of the former Rewley Road depot. Note the Signal & Telegraph engineers working on the gantry and the guard going off duty. The date of this image is 3 March 1961.

Swindon-built 7027 ex GWR Collett '4073' Castle class 4-6-0 No 7023 *Penrice Castle* is pictured leaving Oxford with the afternoon Paddington-Hereford/Worcester express (Cathedrals). The location is where the railway crosses the Oxford Canal and the date was 11 March 1961. Locomotive No 7023 was built under BR in 1949 and withdrawn from service by them in February 1965.

Swindon-built ex GWR '49xx' Hall class 4-6-0 No 4985 *Allesley Hall* is pictured approaching Oxford from the north, with a train of mixed stock in May 1961. Outshopped in January 1931 this loco was withdrawn from service in September 1964. There were 259 Halls built by the GWR between 1928 and 1943 (including a rebuilt Saint class loco as a prototype). Only 258 came into BR stock as loco No 4911 *Bowden Hall* was destroyed in a 1941 air raid. Later 71 Modified Hall 4-6-0s were built (1944 to 1950) making the combined BR total 329 locos. A popular, and purely fanciful, tale passed between youthful enthusiasts during the steam era was that British Railways were considering increasing the number of Halls to 330. In that event the name of the last loco would be *That's all*. Oh happy memories!

BR standard 9F 2-10-0 No 92224 is pictured on the Oxford-Banbury line with an 'Up' freight near Wolvercot Junction in 1961. This loco was built at Crewe in 1958, outshopped in June of that year and withdrawn in September 1967.

BR standard 9F 2-10-0 No 92021 is pictured on shed at Oxford in April 1961. This locomotive was built at Crewe in 1955 entering service in March of that year; it was withdrawn in November 1967. It was one of 10 standard 9Fs fitted with Franco-Crosti boilers ie one normal and one preheat. However the experiment was less than successful and was later discontinued but with the locos retaining the 'Crosti' appearance although reconfigured to operate as normally draughted engines with single boilers.

Ex LMS Stanier 8F 2-8-0 is seen 'on shed' during May 1961. Note that this 1944 Horwich Works-built freight loco is in ex works condition and in all probability had just completed a 'running in' turn from Swindon after receiving attention. This 8F served until being withdrawn in October 1966. Note the 'star' on the cabside (under the number); it denotes that this loco has been 50 per cent reciprocating balanced to facilitate running at higher speeds.

Ex LNWR 'G2' class 0-8-0 'Super D' freight loco is pictured while having the tender tank replenished with water 'on shed' at Oxford in July 1961. This 1922 Crewe-built locomotive was withdrawn by BR in December 1962.

A 1944 Swindon-built Stanier 8F No 48450 is pictured halted at signals to the north of Oxford station while heading a Swindon-Birmingham train of car parts, on 8 May 1961. This loco was withdrawn in September 1967. The 'circular rings' on the signal blades, visible on signals to both sides of the engine, are worthy of note. Rings were fitted to the arms of the goods line signals so that they could continue to be easily distinguished during daylight. The LNWR was the first company to use ringed signal arms. Generally the signal arms applying to goods lines (or slow lines) were fitted with rings, in addition where there were many lines together signals applying to alternate lines were often so fitted.

Ex GWR '43xx' class 2-6-0 (Mogul) no 7327 is pictured in May 1961 passing through Oxford station with an 'Up' freight train. Loco No 9654 a '57xx' 0-6-0PT can just be glimpsed beyond the front of the Churchward 2-6-0. Loco No 7327 was built at Swindon in 1932 and withdrawn by BR in November 1964.

Ex GWR '6959' class Modified Hall No 6960 *Raveningham Hall* is pictured making an energetic departure northbound to Banbury from Oxford station with a horsebox and milk tank train, the date was 13 July 1961. Loco No 6960 was built at Swindon in 1944 and withdrawn in June 1964; it is a preserved engine.

A typical steam era scene at the east end of Oxford station taken on 13 April 1961. Modified Hall 4-6-0 No 7904 *Fountains Hall* (built 1949 and withdrawn 1965) stands alongside ex GWR Castle 4-6-0 No 7005 *Sir Edward Elgar* which had just arrived with the morning Hereford/Worcester-Paddington express. 'Castle' 7005 was built in 1946 and entered traffic in June of that year; the loco worked 869,370 miles in service before being withdrawn in September 1964.

Rebuilt Bulleid 'West Country' class Pacific No 34018 *Axminster* (an engine at that time allocated to (70D) Basingstoke) is seen 'on shed' at Oxford having worked in with a 'Pines Express' during the summer of 1965. This loco was Built at Brighton and entered service for the Southern Region in 1945. The loco was rebuilt in 1958 and withdrawn by BR in April 1968.

Rebuilt Bulleid 'Battle of Britain' class Pacific No 34085 501 *Squadron* 'gets the road' at Oxford station with a southbound 'Pines Express' working. This loco was built at Brighton by BR and entered service in December 1948 it was rebuilt in June 1960 and withdrawn in April 1966.

Works outing July 1961 style. BR Standard 'Class 5' 5MT 4-6-0 No 73161 is pictured leaving Oxford with the return working 'Appleyard of Leeds' works special. This BR Standard was built at Derby in 1956 and entered service in the November of that year; it was withdrawn from service in March 1968. Loco No 73161 was one of 30 of the class of 172 fitted with Caprotti valve gear.

Ex works condition! BR Standard 'Class 4' 4MT 4-6-0 No 75007 is pictured in tip top order 'on shed' at Oxford on 16 June 1962, probably following a 'running in' turn, having received attention at Swindon Works. Note the huge lump of coal at the front of the 'over full' tender and also the concertina weather sheet fitted between loco and tender. Loco No 75007 was built at Swindon in 1951 and entered traffic in September of that year the loco being withdrawn from service in April 1965

Chapter 7

PATRIOT –
THE UNKNOWN
WARRIOR

In March 2009 a group of dedicated enthusiasts took delivery of a set of
newly cut locomotive frame plates. Perhaps not an earth-shattering piece of
information when viewed in isolation but add in all the other salient facts
and you will appreciate what a great railway preservation milestone the cutting
of those steel frames represents.

They were purchased by members of the LMS-Patriot Company Ltd, who
with the help of public donations, have commenced the building of a completely
new steam locomotive to be entirely representative of the long defunct
5XP/6P5F 'Patriot Class', in original build form. They plan to 'steam' that new
engine well in time for the '100th Anniversary of the Armistice' in 2018,
poignantly the new Patriot 4-6-0 No 45551 will be named *The Unknown
Warrior*.

In October 2008, the order for the frame plates was placed with Corus Steel.
Measuring 39ft in length 4ft high and 1⅛ in thick, the two steel frame plates
gave the new 'Patriot' locomotive an official identity for the first time. The
frame plates were plasma cut to the correct shape and then machined and
drilled. Thereafter they were delivered to the Llangollen Railway Works in
Spring 2009, where the assembly of locomotive No 5551 will be carried out.
You could say that the group are following in a certain Mr Fowler's footsteps,
albeit some 79 years later!

'Patriot' class 4-6-0 No 45544 backing out of Liverpool Lime Street on 16 July 1955. This is one of only 10 'Patriots' that were unnamed. Loco No 45544 was built at Crewe and entered service in March 1944, it was never rebuilt and was withdrawn by BR in November 1961. Dick Blenkinsop/The LMS-Patriot Project

Patriot 4-6-0 No 45506 *The Royal Pioneer Corps* is seen at Crewe Works on 27 May 1956 after an overhaul. This locomotive was built at Crewe Works in 1932 and named in 1948; this engine was never rebuilt and it was withdrawn by BR in March 1962. TB Owen/The LMS-Patriot Project

'Patriot' 4-6-0 No 45546 *Fleetwood* is pictured with a Liverpool/Manchester express near Symington on the WCML, 14 June 1958. Built at Crewe in 1934 this loco was withdrawn by BR June 1962. David Anderson

Sir Henry Fowler

First then let us examine the origin of the ex LMS 'Patriot Class'. Almost all British-built steam locomotive classes are directly linked to the name of a designer and in the case of the Patriots that name is Sir Henry Fowler (1870-1938). The Henry Fowler name could well have been linked with fine furniture and not railway locomotives, had the Evesham-born young Fowler chosen to follow in his father's footsteps and become a cabinet maker. He instead chose locomotive engineering and became an apprentice under John Aspinall (later Sir John) at the Horwich Works of the Lancashire & Yorkshire Railway.

In 1900 Fowler joined the Midland Railway eventually becoming assistant works manager at Derby in 1905 and works manager two years later. Fowler served as Chief Mechanical Engineer of the Midland Railway (MR) from 1909 to 1922, and then the London Midland & Scottish Railway (LMSR) from 1925 to 1930. He previously served the LMSR as deputy CME under George Hughes and to his credit designed the highly successful 'Royal Scot' class.

He was bestowed with a knighthood for wartime service (1914-1918) to the railways. Interestingly after completing his term as CME, Fowler became adviser to the LMS research department's vice-president (1931 to 1933) and in that capacity he oversaw the purchase of various prototype diesel shunting locomotives, a great many of which were later introduced into traffic by the company.

The leader of the class 4-6-0 No 45500 *Patriot* pictured at speed on the WCML near Symington with a Glasgow Liverpool/Manchester express on 25 June 1960. Note the driving wheels with large centre bosses, inherited from the LNWR 'Claughton' class loco it replaced. Loco 5500 originally carried the name and number of the Claughton No 5971 *Croxteth*, when introduced by the LMS in November 1930. It was renumbered in 1935 and subsequently renamed *Patriot* in 1937. The loco was never rebuilt and was withdrawn by BR in March 1961. David Anderson

BW 'Patriot' class 4-6-0 No 45513, an unnamed loco with 'normal' Patriot LMS wheelsets is pictured at the same location in June 1960. Loco number 45513 was built at Crewe in 1932, this engine was never rebuilt and was withdrawn by BR in September 1962. David Anderson

Birth of the 'Baby Scots'

During the late 1920s Fowler was occupied with trying to improve the performance of an earlier London North Western Railway design of 4-6-0 passenger locomotives known as the 'Claughton' class. The four-cylinder front line Crewe-built express locomotives never consistently delivered good performances in traffic. By 1928 Fowler had tried several modifications including the fitting of larger boilers, but despite the modifications the 'Claughtons' remained erratic performers.

In 1930 the LMS took a decision to rebuild two of the Claughton class locos as three-cylinder engines with three sets of Walschaert valve gear. Fowler decided to incorporate long travel valves and the improved 1928 parallel boiler design; in addition the driving wheels of the Claughtons were re-used but in truth little else. The rebuilt 4-6-0 locomotives were No 5971 *Croxteth* and No 5902 *Sir Frank Ree*; both at that time retained their original name and number. The work was carried out at Derby Works.

Unlike the 'Claughton' class the new locomotives were a great success and because of their close physical resemblance to the slightly larger and more powerful Fowler 'Royal Scot' class (but with lower axle loading) the new engines became colloquially known as 'Baby Scots'. Those lineside enthusiasts of the 1940s and 50s who are honest, will admit to on more than one occasion shouting 'It's a Scot' to their colleagues only to realise seconds later that the approaching loco was in fact a 'Baby Scot'! Instant loco class identification got even trickier in later times when fast-approaching rebuilt Scots, Pats and Jubs, all looked similar at first glance!

Following the early success of the first two rebuilt engines the LMS embarked in 1932 upon a building programme of 50 more 'Baby Scot' locomotives, 40 at Crewe Works and 10 at Derby Works; the two batches were constructed

This picture of Patriot 4-6-0 No 45503 *The Royal Leicestershire Regiment* over the ash pit at Edinburgh Dalry Road shed (taken on 14 July 1955) illustrates well the similarity of the class with 'Royal Scot' class engines, justifying the name 'Baby Scot'. Loco No 45503 was built at Crewe in 1932; this engine was never rebuilt and was withdrawn by BR in August 1961. David Anderson

simultaneously. The Chief Mechanical Engineer of the LMS at that time being Sir Ernest Lemon (1931-1932) who was succeeded by Sir William Stanier (1932 to 1944).

The first 40 engines were designated as rebuilds of the life-expired 'Claughton' class. However the term 'rebuild' in that instance was probably used for accounting purposes only. For although 'as built' the new locos carried the names and numbers of the Claughton 4-6-0s they replaced, few if any actual parts of the former LNWR locos were used in their construction. The last ten engines were officially designated as 'new build'.

Five more of the class, to be numbered 5552 to 5556, were ordered from Crewe Works in 1934 but in the event those locomotives were alternatively built to a Stanier design with taper boilers and top feeds, effectively becoming the first of the 4-6-0 'Jubilee Class' classified as built '5XP' and then in 1951 reclassified as '6P5F'.

In 1935 the class was renumbered by the LMS, with numbers 5500 to 5541 being allocated to the supposed rebuilds, and numbers 5542 to 5551 allocated to the officially categorised 'new' engines. Only after the naming of loco No 5500 as Patriot in February 1937 (originally called *Croxteth*) did the then '5XP' 4-6-0 class take on the designation of 'Patriot Class'. The whole of the class were not given names and indeed some names were changed.

Patriots in service

Originally the 'Patriot' class locomotives were not considered to be the exact equal of the 'Royal Scot' class and were therefore classified as '5XP', the same category as the two-cylinder LMS 5MT 'Black Five' class. The power classification for the unrebuilt 'Patriots' was changed to '6P5F' in 1951 by British Railways. The 'Patriots' were to be seen at work hauling a great many of the express passenger services on the Midland Division of the LMS. Notably the class regularly worked the frequent London Euston-Birmingham New Street two-hour expresses.

Paired with a Fowler 3500-gallon tender (5½ tons of coal with greedy rails) the newly introduced 'Patriots' performed well and were highly regarded

Opposite: Patriot 4-6-0 No 45504 *Royal Signals* is pictured c1960. This loco was built at Crewe in 1932 and was not rebuilt; withdrawn by BR in March 1962.
Author

engines by the crews who worked them. They soon established a reputation as fast runners and reports of speeds in the region of 93mph were not uncommon. In fact in regular traffic the class often took on jobs normally rostered for the larger and more highly rated 'Royal Scots', and were never proved to be in any way inferior to that class.

After the formation of British Railways, 'Patriot' class engines (including rebuilt versions) could be found mainly at depots associated with the West Coast Main Line with a small allocation at the BR LMR Leeds depot. Later members of the class were allocated to other locations to suit changing traffic patterns.

Patriot 4-6-0 No 45509 *The Derbyshire Yeomanry* **is seen at Gloucester Eastgate with a train from Birmingham New Street to Bristol on a very foggy morning, 18 November 1953. Loco No 45509 was built at Crewe in 1932, this engine was never rebuilt and was withdrawn by BR in August 1961. Dick Blenkinsop/The LMS-Patriot Project**

Patriot 4-6-0 No 45517 (unnamed) is pictured taking water 'on the move' at Whitmore Troughs with an 'up' train on 3 August 1957. This loco was built at Crewe in 1933 and was never rebuilt; it was withdrawn by BR in June 1962. **Dick Blenkinsop/The LMS-Patriot Project**

1948 'Patriot' class locomotive allocations							
1A Willesden	3B Bushbury	5A Crewe North	8A Edge Hill	9A Longsight	10B Preston	12A Carlisle Upperby	20A Leeds Holbeck
3 Locos 45509/10/ 25	5 Locos 45514/28/ 29/31/40	14 Locos 45503/04/ 07/08/11/ 12/22/32/ 39/42/46/ 48/49/51	12 Locos 45500/01/ 17/20/21/23 /26/27/33/ 43/45/47	1 Loco 45530	10 Locos 45502/05/ 13/15/16/ 19/24/36/ 37/44	4 Locos 45506/18 /41/50	3 Locos 45534/35 /38

Unrebuilt 4-6-0 'Patriot' class. Year end locomotive totals, in BR service							
1948	1950	1960	1961	1962	1963	1964	1965
35 Locos	34 Locos	32 Locos	24 Locos	Nil	Nil	Nil	Nil
First locomotive of the type to be withdrawn was No 45502 in September 1960, and the last was No 45550 in November 1962							

Patriot 4-6-0 No 45547 (unnamed) is pictured having just past Shotton station on the North Wales main line on 18 February 1961. Loco No 45547 was built at Crewe in 1934 and was never rebuilt: it was withdrawn by BR in September 1962. Dick Blenkinsop/The LMS-Patriot Project

Patriot No 45551 – The Unknown Warrior

The creation of new build main line steam locomotives using modern engineering techniques and traditional locomotive building materials has post-*Tornado* been accepted as being viable. Perhaps the most difficult part of any such project is raising the relatively large amounts of money required to pay for materials and help to fund the construction. Highlighting the importance of money in no way detracts from the importance of the volunteer element, not just with the actual 'engineering work' but in dealing with, and overcoming, a whole host of ancillary challenges.

The completion and steaming of loco No 60163 *Tornado* in 2008 not only proved that 'it can be done' but succeeded in selling the idea of building a modern-day living breathing steam locomotive to a population who were perhaps hungry for a new object of national pride. After all what's wrong with 'Made in Britain', furthermore what could be more British in origin than a steam locomotive? Where Tornado has gone before others will follow, in addition to *The Unknown Warrior* there were six other new build steam locomotive projects under way as we entered 2009.

Left: March 2009. The frames for 45551 are seen being laser cut at the works of Corus Steel. Andrew Laws/The LMS-Patriot Project

March 2009. The 'cut' frames are seen awaiting final drilling before delivery to Llangollen Railway. **Andrew Laws/The LMS-Patriot Project**

All such projects are supported by the collective will of the railway preservation movement, the driving force of the individual building group and most importantly, in all cases they rely on the financial support of the great British public. During the building of *The Unknown Warrior* dying engineering skills will be revived. Yet fascinatingly many of those working on this project, either directly or indirectly, are too young to have had any first-hand experience of the steam era, such is the enduring and magnetic attraction of steam power.

There are a great many 'gaps' in British steam preservation in fact from the 1948 BR locomotive stock list of approximately 500 steam locomotive classes and sub-classes only some 117 types are represented. On the basis of personal preference the non-representation of classes will be viewed differently. But few would dispute that the inspired decision to build a representative of the iconic ex LNER 4-6-2 A1 class became an achievement which caught the imagination of countless thousands of people, the majority of which were not necessarily dyed-in-the-wool railway enthusiasts!

Waiting for the road. The driver of Ex LMS Patriot No 45516 *The Bedfordshire and Hertfordshire Regiment* is pictured waiting for the right away from Manchester Exchange Station in February 1959. This loco was built at Crewe in 1932 and was never rebuilt; it was withdrawn by BR in August 1961. Author's Collection

Public Interest

What then of the decision to build a new Patriot? Will that worthy venture also attract the imagination of the public? Initial indications are that it will. As an enthusiast you could argue that it will complete an LMS set, given the historic links between the ex LMS 4-6-0 classes of 'Patriot', 'Royal Scot' and 'Jubilee'. There are four preserved 6P5F Jubilees and two restored 7P Royal Scots, however no 'Patriot' class engines (of either type) survived into preservation. The choice of original build and not rebuilt type for the 'new build' makes the project very special indeed, for not only will the new 'Baby Scot' represent its own class it will (in those of an age) engender memories of the original parallel boiler 'Royal Scot' class.

David Bradshaw, the current chairman of the project, is a man whose name can be directly linked with another new build locomotive namely the GWR 'County'. To his credit he is also the originator of the 'Patriot Project'. David's enthusiasm for the class was stirred by youthful memories of seeing 'Baby Scots' at work in and around his native Shropshire. Now in 2009 his early thoughts and wishes are on the way to being realised.

Having been told of the 'Patriot' idea by David established railway preservation journalist Tony Streeter, became an instant convert to the cause. With his help the steam railway press were made aware of the idea, which they happily presented to their readers. It soon became apparent that David Bradshaw was not the only steam enthusiast to cherish the idea of creating a new 'Patriot' locomotive.

In their hundreds the readers of those journals in particular and the preservation movement in general, were intrigued by the thought of creating such a locomotive from scratch. After the initial magazine articles there followed further publicity at preserved railway events and it seemed back then that just about everyone who supports railway preservation was talking about the fascinating 'Patriot' proposal. Around midsummer 2007 the 'Patriot Project' received more good media coverage and as a result public interest was further heightened. The formal launch of the 'Patriot Project' came in April 2008, in the form of a well-attended 'Patriot Gala' event held at the Llangollen Railway.

The project gathers momentum

David Bradshaw takes up the story: "For perhaps the first time in new build history we have used modern communication technology to help spread the word and gather support. Our website, which was set up through Andrew Laws who is now our Marketing and Publicity Director and incidentally was our first volunteer, is crucial to the ongoing success of the project. In addition we now have a steady stream of support flowing in via email and post; to help with that work Richard Sant joined our growing band of helpers, Richard is now our Company Secretary.

"By this time it had become abundantly clear that there was sufficient support to begin the serious business of building a new engine. Richard funded and organised the creation of a charitable company, and later set up the all-important membership scheme. I managed to get hold of a number of key drawings through the assistance of Bob Essery of the Bahamas Locomotive Society, and also from the archives of the National Railway Museum. Additional new drawings have also been created by Pete Rich and Fred James, for extra clarity and to fill in where originals simply do not exist.

"At that period we were successful in persuading the Vale of Glamorgan Council to agree to the derelict, but nevertheless largely complete, Fowler 3500-gallon tender at Barry being donated to the project, subject only to its restoration being carried out at Barry. Thanks must also go to John Buxton of Cambrian Transport Ltd for his support from the beginning of the project both with the negotiations for the tender and for looking after the all important donations to the project before the formation of the 'LMS-Patriot Company Ltd' was completed. What was then still lacking was someone to look after engineering and we were fortunate in being introduced to Steve Blackburn, formerly of Crewe Works, who recently became our Engineering Director and has responsibility for quality management and engineering liaison.

"Money had started to come in and so it became evident that we needed to get something physical done to convince our supporters that this was not a flash in the pan, so we agreed that we must give a number and name to the proposed new locomotive. To facilitate that an appeal was made via the steam railway press. As there was no possibility of a new number (as with the A1) because the new build Stanier Jubilees took the next number in the LMS sequence ie No 45552, we agreed that No 45551 was probably the best bet.

"We didn't want to create a replica 45500 because that engine was more of a Claughton rebuild and differed in a number of significant areas from the other production Patriot engines. Following receipt of around 150 possible names for the new engine we selected the five most popular and put those to a public vote. The winner by some distance was 'The Unknown Warrior'. John Buxton of Cambrian Transport, our first commercial sponsor, paid for three nameplates which were duly cast by Newton replicas as was the smokebox number plate which in turn was sponsored by member Neil Kinsey. The winner of the naming competition was Kevin Finnerty, he is now a director of the company with specific responsibility for history and archives.

"On the engineering front we agreed that the erection of the engine would be placed in the hands of Dave Owen a director and Chief Mechanical Engineer of the Llangollen Railway. I contacted Pete Rich who agreed to produce the frame drawings from the frame arrangement drawings supplied to us by the Bahamas team. The frames were duly ordered from Corus and delivered to Cradley Heath in late 2008 where they cut to shape in March 2009. They were then drilled by The Boro' Foundry and then delivered to the Llangollen Railway. The birth of the 53rd 'Patriot' has thus taken place.

"We have acquired a set of 3ft 3½ in diameter bogie wheels from ex Barry 10 Stanier '8F' No 48518 and hope to obtain a second wheelset following the repatriation of four more 8Fs from Turkey. There also exists a pattern for the 6ft 9in diameter driving wheels (identical to those of the 'Jubilee' class) and which were used to cast the new driving wheelset for No 45699 'Galatea'. We remain hopeful that we can negotiate a deal with Tyseley Locomotive Works (the owners of the pattern) to allow its use for the LMS-Patriot Project.

A Glasgow Central to Blackpool North Relief Excursion pictured at Crawford on the WCML in July 1960. Loco No 45517 was unnamed and built at Crewe in 1933 being withdrawn by BR in June 1962.
David Anderson

"The frames will hopefully be completed by the end of 2009 when we will need to embark upon a massive fund-raising exercise in order to 'wheel' the engine; a cost for that work in the region of £160,000 is anticipated. The LMS-Patriot Project raises money through regular monthly donations from supporters, and has also received some significant single donations from LMS enthusiasts. These donations have been supplemented by Gift Aid, where the Government contributes an extra 25 per cent of the donation, from UK taxpayers. We also seeking further corporate sponsors and are looking to raise income from legacies.

National Memorial engine

"In January 2009, we had talks in London with Stuart Gendall, Director of Corporate Communications at the Royal British Legion. The LMS-Patriot Project obtained endorsement from the Royal British Legion (an internationally known charity) which helps servicemen and women through its annual Poppy Appeal. The LMS-Patriot Project sought recognition in creating a new National Memorial engine, dedicated to the memory of fallen servicemen and women. The RBL's involvement will bring the project to a wider audience and hopefully will inspire a new generation of steam enthusiasts.

"The *Tornado* Project has now captured the general public's imagination, whilst proving that new build steam locomotives can be successfully built in the UK. In building loco No 45551 the LMS-Patriot Project will fashion a new icon, a machine which will be more than just another steam locomotive. The new 'Patriot' class loco will be a fitting memorial and remembrance engine for the 21st century, in the same way that the original No 45500 'Patriot' was a memorial in the 20th century to all the brave men and women who fought and died for their country in the Great War."

Rebuilt Patriots

In 1942 the LMS rebuilt two Jubilee 7P 4-6-0 locomotives, numbers (4)5735 and (4)5736; they were rebuilt with larger boilers, double chimneys and smoke deflectors. The design was hailed as being a great success and so led directly to the rebuilding of 18 members of the 'Patriot' class to an Ivatt design between 1946 and 1949. Thus some 'Patriot' rebuilds were LMS-built engines (eight locos) and others British Railways engines (10 locos), ie built after January 1948.

The locos were rebuilt with the larger Stanier 2A taper boilers, double chimneys, new cylinders, new cabs and new tenders and later they were fitted with curved 'Scot' type smoke deflectors. When newly built the 'Patriots' were given the power classification 7P. In service the rebuilt 'Patriot' locos were considered to be equal in performance to the rebuilt 'Royal Scot' locomotives and additionally were described as 'much better riding engines'. In general terms the 'Patriot' rebuilds were hardly distinguishable from the rebuilt Royal Scots and rebuilt Jubilees.

Rebuilt Patriot 4-6-0 No 45529 *Stephenson* with an 'up' relief at Denbigh Hall Bletchley on 27 July 1963. Built at Crewe in 1933 this loco was rebuilt in 1947 and withdrawn by BR in February 1964 having run 1,543,356 miles during 31 years of service. David Anderson

Rebuilt 4-6-0 'Patriot' class. Year end locomotive totals, in BR service							
1948	1950	1960	1961	1962	1963	1964	1965
17 Locos	18 Locos	18 Locos	17 Locos	16 Locos	11 Locos	3 Locos	Nil
First locomotive of the type to be withdrawn was No 45514 in May 1961, and the last was No 45531 in November 1965.							

- The eight LMS 'Patriot' rebuilds were numbers 5514, 5521, 5526, 5528, 5529, 5530, 5531 and 5540 (LMS numbers).
- The 10 BR 'Patriot' rebuilds were numbers 45512, 45522, 45523, 45525, 45527, 45532, 45534, 45535, 45536 and 45545 (BR numbers).

Rebuilt Patriot 4-6-0 No 45530 *Sir Frank Ree* is pictured adjacent to the coaling plant and among the railway 'clutter' that was Willesden steam depot. The 1933 Crewe built loco was pictured on 5 May 1964, note that the name plates are already missing even though this loco was not withdrawn until December 1965. Author's Collection

Rebuilt *Patriot* class loco No 45522 Prestatyn is pictured at Dore in 1963 and was at the time looking a little the worse for wear. The 1933 Derby built engine was rebuilt in January 1949 and withdrawn by BR in September 1964.

Rebuilt Patriot 4-6-0 No 45534 *E.Tootal Broadhurst* pictured 'on shed' at Llandudno Junction in 1962. This loco was built at Derby in 1933, rebuilt in 1948 and withdrawn by BR in May 1964. Author's Collection

Rebuilt Patriot 4-6-0 No 45521 *Rhyl* pictured being turned at Morecambe in June 1963. This loco was built at Derby in 1933, rebuilt in 1946 and withdrawn by BR in September 1963. Author's Collection

Rebuilt Patriot 4-6-0 No 45522 *Prestatyn* pictured 'on shed' at Buxton in 1964. This loco was built at Derby in 1933, rebuilt in 1949 and withdrawn by BR in September 1964. Author's Collection

Ex LMS Patriot 4-6-0 Locomotive Specification. Number Series BR 45500-45551		
	Patriot	**Rebuilt Patriot**
Power Classification	5XP/6P5F*	6P/7P*
Introduced	1930/1934	1946/49
Designer	Fowler	Fowler/Ivatt rebuilds
Company	LMS	LMS/BR LMR
Driving Wheel	6ft 9in	6ft 9in
Boiler Pressure	200psi Superheated	250psi Superheated
Cylinders	Three 18in x 26in	Three 17in x 26in
Tractive Effort	26520lbf	29570lbf
Valve Gear	26520lbf	29570lbf
*Reclassified 1951.		

Rebuilt 'Patriot' 4-6-0 No 45512 *Bunsen* pictured at Hatch End in June 1964. Loco No 45512 was built at Crewe and entered service in September 1932, was rebuilt in July 1948 and withdrawn by BR in March 1965. Author's Collection

Rebuilt 'Jubilee' 4-6-0 No 45735 *Comet* pictured at Euston Station on a very wet September day in 1963. Loco No 45735 was built at Crewe in 1936 and rebuilt in 1942, being withdrawn by BR in September 1964. Author's Collection

Rebuilt 'Royal Scot' 4-6-0 No 46152 *The King's Dragoon Guardsman* (the identity swap Royal Scot loco, see relevant chapter this publication) is pictured at Chester General Station in August 1958. Author's Collection

Chapter 8

MAIN LINE – STEAM FOCUS

Fred Kerr

My interest in railways started in the early 1950s when living in Edinburgh. As a family we used the Caledonian suburban lines from Leith North to Edinburgh Princes Street (the 'Caley' station) regularly and often taking the opportunity to spend time in Princes Street Gardens. There was a lot for the enthusiast to see and enjoy, passengers trains to and from Glasgow and Inverness, a whole host of local suburban services and perhaps best of all what seemed like constant convoys of locomotives working between the busy shed at Haymarket and the even busier Waverley station.

My grandparents lived in Birmingham accordingly I made several family trips south via the West Coast Main Line. My mother's parents lived equidistant from (and within hearing distance of) Acocks Green and Hall Green stations; I got my introduction to GWR locomotives. Tucked up in bed on a summer's night, with the window open, I could hear the distant whistles of GWR engines and often tried to imagine what loco type a particular whistle represented.

In 1956 my parents moved to Corby where for the first time I became familiar with heavy freight trains, seeing my first Beyer Garrett at that time. Visits to see locos at work within the industrial complex of the 'then' steel giants Stewarts & Lloyds are another lasting memory. Pen Green loco shed at Corby works was some place, with room for 40 locomotives. I recall observing mainly saddle tanks, always hard at work.

In 1960 my photography interest proper began, thanks to a cousin who bought me a 'Brownie 127' as a Christmas present. Soon after starting work in 1964 I upgraded to a 35mm Minolta camera however the price of film and processing, compared with my weekly wage of £5 meant that I tended to make a film last a very long time! Black and white photography was the economical option of the day.

Gaining a university place in the 1970s I got to meet with other photographers and was able to try out a variety of cameras. Apart from the obvious higher education did have its advantages; I was able to use the university's darkroom for my processing. I later became a staff photographer for the student newspaper, a move that gave me unlimited access to the darkrooms at any time, day or night. Oh happy days.

Upon leaving university I joined the civil service and moved to London. Upgrading my photographic kit again I settled on a Pentax 6x7, with which I had good results for over a decade. Shutter problems with the Pentax unfortunately occurred, which I discovered would not be cost effective to repair. Thus an enforced change meant that I bought a Bronica 645 kit, which I still have.

I made the switch to digital in 2001 when I bought a Fuji 6900, a good camera with which to learn the 'digital way'. Later I upgraded first to a Nikon D100 and then a Nikon D300, which is now my basic camera. I abandoned film altogether in 2004 and now work exclusively in digital, a format which has huge advantages both over the actual creation of images and importantly in enormous cost savings.

My long-standing interest in railway photography is not just the locomotives (or modern units) themselves but the whole railway infrastructure. In endeavouring to create an image which emphasises the power of the loco I also attempt to show the railway environment which 'it' operates within, be that the steel 'clutter' of the modern high speed line or the branches of a tree.

My present everyday track side photography kit consists of a Nikon D300 body with Nikon 18-55mm f3.5/5.6, 24-120 f3.5/5.6, 35-70 f2.8 and 80-200 f2.8 zoom lenses. I hope you enjoy this selection of main line steam locomotives at work. Fred Kerr, May 2009.

Opposite: During 2007 Stanier 'Princess Royal Class' 8P 4-6-2 No 6201 *Princess Elizabeth* was based at the East Lancashire Railway. On 28 July 2007 it was chartered as motive power for a tour organised by John Fishwick Travel, from Manchester Victoria to Carlisle via the S&C and is seen powering away from the West Coast Main Line at Lostock Hall.

Pictured on 21 February 2004 a great pairing of locomotives working a Manchester-Carlisle charter (carrying a Pines Express headboard), using Standard 'Class 4' 2-6-0 No 76079 (in the guise of scrapped sister engine No 76029) piloting Bulleid Battle of Britain Class 7P6F 4-6-2 No 34067 Tangmere, seen powering off Ribblehead Viaduct on the return journey. Loco No 76079 was built by BR at Horwich in 1957 and withdrawn in November 1967. Bulleid Pacific No 34067 was built for Southern Railways at Brighton in 1947 and withdrawn by BR in November 1963.

In March 2006 those enthusiasts prepared to brave the cold were rewarded with the glorious spectacle of snow, sunshine, and steam as Stanier Class '5MT 4-6-0 'No 45407 and Standard 'Class 4' 2-6-0 No 76079 breasted the summit at Copy Pit with a charter run from Liverpool Lime St.

The beginning of 2004 sees Standard 'Class 4' 2-6-0 No 76079 hard at work as it pilots 'Battle of Britain' Class 7P6F 4-6-2 No 34067 *Tangmere* on the approach to Copy Pit summit, pictured on 3 January 2004 while working the Manchester-Morecambe stage of a railtour emanating from Northampton.

Separated by only a few miles and two hours from the snowy scene at Copy Pit, Stanier 'Class 5' 4-6-0 No 45407 pilots 'Standard Class 4' 2-6-0 No 76079 past Chapeltown on the Blackburn-Bolton direct line with a charter tour from Liverpool Lime St. Stanier 'Black Five' No 45407 (LMS 5407) was built for the LMS by Armstrong Whitworth & Co Ltd and entered service in September 1937 being withdrawn at the end of the BR steam era in August 1968.

Rebuilt 'Royal Scot' 4-6-0 No 46115 *Scots Guardsman* made an unexpected return to service on 29 November 2008 when it substituted for Maunsell Lord Nelson Class 8P 4-6-0 No 850 *Lord Nelson* which had been scheduled to work a Carnforth-Scarborough charter as part of its main line approval. On the night before the charter was due to operate Network Rail decided that 850 was out of gauge and 46115 was hurriedly 'fired up' to work the train. The morning of the charter was one of perfect winter conditions as shown by these scenes of 46115 powering away from Hellifield after its water stop at Longpreston with its exhaust hanging in the frosty air. Loco No 46115 in original form was built for the LMS by the North British Locomotive Co Ltd in 1927 and withdrawn from service by BR in December 1965.

"We do like to be beside the seaside" especially when it brings a steam locomotive to visit! On 10 May 2008 Stanier Duchess 4-6-2 No 6233 *Duchess of Sutherland* worked a charter from the Midlands to Blackpool and was caught on camera accelerating from a signal check at Euxton on the return journey south. Note the 'steelwork' associated with modern high speed electrified lines.

The new 'mainline' A1 Pacific *Tornado* is pictured running on the short demonstration line during the Barrow Hill LNER Gala held in April 2009.

Below: In July 2008 the National Railway Museum celebrated the 70th anniversary of Gresley Class 'A4 '8P 4-6-2 No 4468 *Mallard* achieving the World Record speed of 126mph in 1938, by bringing together three main line certified locomotives to join 4468 for a weekend display in the NRM yard. The three main line locomotives also worked stages of a two-day London-Edinburgh charter hauled throughout by 'A4' Pacifics. Loco No 60019 *Bittern* is seen passing Colton Junction on 6 July on the York-London stage of the tour. Built for the LNER at Doncaster in 1937 No 60019 was withdrawn by BR in September 1966.

Left: Once it had gained its main line certificate in 2008 Gresley Class 'A4' 8P No 4-6-2 60007 *Sir Nigel Gresley* became a welcome visitor to the Settle &Carlisle route. The locomotive was pictured leaving Appleby following a scheduled stop. Loco No 60007 was built at Doncaster for the LNER and entered service in November 1937, being withdrawn by BR in February 1966.

This optical illusion creates the impression of speed record holder *Mallard* in steam, but alas the smoke is from sister engine No 60019 *Bittern*. The occasion was the July 2008 the NRM inspired *Mallard* 'Speed Record 70th Anniversary' celebration.

In 2008 'Standard Class 7' 4-6-2 No 70013 *Oliver Cromwell* was restored to main line condition so that it would be available to take its part in celebrations to mark the 40th anniversary of the end of steam on BR, in 1968. The superbly turned out National Collection locomotive is pictured 'on shed' at Carnforth.

Before being allowed on the main line, newly overhauled locomotives spend some time on a suitable heritage line to accumulate mileage and iron out any niggling faults which may be found. Recently overhauled Gresley A4 Class 4-6-2 No 60007 *Sir Nigel Gresley* spent time on the North Yorkshire Moors Railway where it was photographed on 12 March 2008 while making a series of runpasts out of Goathland when being used for a photographic charter.

In April 2008 the North Yorks Moors Railway decided to hold an LNER Weekend with the main attraction being the use of three Class 'A4' Pacific locomotives plus the NRM's Class 'V2' No 4771 *Green Arrow*. Pictured at Grosmont shed are 'A4' No 60009 *Union of South Africa* with a Grosmont-Pickering service, the 'out of service' No 4771 and 'A4' No 60007 which was being prepared for its next duty.

'Standard Class 7' 4-6-2 No 70013 *Oliver Cromwell* ran at the Great Central Railway as locomotive No 70048 *The Territorial Army 1908-1958* for a short while to commemorate the Centenary of that force. The loco however carried a modified nameplate reading *The Territorial Army 1908-2008*. The 'Standard Pacific' was photographed at Woodhouse on the GCR while in that temporary guise.

One of the NRM flagship locomotives is Gresley Class 'V2' 7MT 2-6-2 No 4771 *Green Arrow* (BR 60800). On 30 September 2006, shortly before its main line certificate expired, the V2 was operated in its LNER guise as 4771 in apple-green livery and is seen passing Lunds on the Settle & Carlisle route with a northbound charter. Loco No 4771 was built at Doncaster for the LNER and entered service in June 1936, being withdrawn by BR in August 1962.

Before being permitted to run on the main line steam locomotives need to undergo a proving run. On 25 August 2004 'Standard Class 8' 4-6-2 No 71000 *Duke of Gloucester* passed Longpreston while undergoing its test run on the 'Carnforth Circle'. Built by BR at Crewe in 1954 loco No 71000 was withdrawn in November 1962.

Chapter 9

IRISH STEAM – BELFAST-DUBLIN

The Great Northern Railway was Ireland's second largest railway company which at its peak was responsible for a little over 600 route miles of track. The GNR infrastructure included the line probably best known to those outside the island of Ireland, the Belfast-Dublin route. That rail corridor and the commuter Dublin Area Rapid Transit (Dart) line, connecting Dublin with the delightful seaside town of Howth are the only sections of the old GNR system which are still used by regular passenger services.

The GNR was formed in 1876 following a merger between three companies, the Irish North Western Railway, the Northern Railway of Ireland and the Ulster Railway. The GNR developed to become Ireland's most prosperous railway company. Comparisons were often drawn between the GNR Ireland and the GNR England with the Irish railway being seen as copying the image of its English counterpart when it chose apple green livery for its engines and varnished teak wood finish for its coaches. In later times the company chose to use light blue liveried locomotives which had their running gear and frames painted scarlet.

The main line between Ireland's two major cities was well served by the GNR. The Belfast-Dublin 'Enterprise' train service (a survivor of the steam age) still operates daily between those two great cities, although now of course it is diesel powered. For a short while the 'Enterprise' steam timetable was extended to include Cork but that service never attracted the volume of passengers enjoyed by the Belfast-Dublin trains. In addition to the main 'inter city' route the GNR operated services to a large part of the north west of the

'Class V' No 85 *Merlin* has been preserved by the Ulster Folk and Transport Museum. The engine was leased by the Railway Preservation Society of Ireland in the late 1980s to be restored to operational condition and used on the main line. Merlin returned to traffic in 1986. Another major overhaul was performed in the 1990s, and the engine was last used in 2004. It is currently at the RPSI's main base in Whitehead, County Antrim. Pictured leaving Dublin Heuston station with a recreation of the Dublin-Cork 'Enterprise' service. Brian Sharpe

island which, in addition to trains from Belfast, included trains from Dundalk to Derry and from Newry to Bundoran. Other centres of population served by the GNR included Antrim, Clones, Enniskillen, Letterkenny, Omagh, Portadown and Strabane.

In 1921 the partition of Ireland created an international frontier through the GNR's territory. In addition to crossing the Belfast-Dublin route the border dissected two other major and several secondary GNR railway lines. Express cross-border passenger services were affected by the creation of the frontier after which all trains were required to stop for passenger passport control and inspection etc at Dundalk in the south of Ireland and at Goraghwood in the north. However changes were implemented in 1947 when special immigration facilities were opened at Dublin Amiens Street station (renamed in 1966 as Dublin Connolly), and at Belfast Great Victoria Street station to facilitate the smooth running of the 'Enterprise' inter city service.

An upsurge in rail usage during the early part of the 20th century created a need for modern powerful locomotives which the GNR at first wanted to satisfy by the introduction of express 4-6-0 types, something which the Great Southern & Western Railway in the south of the country had successfully done. The main works of the GNR was at Dundalk and it transpired that the lifting shop at that facility was too short to handle larger 4-6-0 locomotives. There was also a weight restriction problem to be taken into consideration at Boyne Bridge near Dundalk. Accordingly the GNR decided to pursue the introduction of a 4-4-0 light axle loading, but nevertheless powerful, loco design to handle their heaviest express trains.

GNR 'Class V' 4-4-0 No 85 _Merlin_ is pictured on 10 September 1959 departing from Lisburn with a Belfast-Dublin excursion. David Anderson

To solve their problem the company in 1932 turned to Beyer Peacock who produced for them a very powerful 4-4-0 three-cylinder compound to a George T Glover design, the first of that type to see service in Ireland. Classified as 'Class V' the 1932-built engines were a great success; the tenders for them were built at the GNR's Dundalk Works. They were rebuilt with Belpaire boilers between 1946 and 1950 and one of the class No 85 *Merlin* is preserved and has regularly worked special trains. However at the beginning of 2009 the loco was 'out of boiler ticket', with no plans in place for an immediate return to steam.

In October 1958 the old GNR (then the Great Northern Railway Board) was split between Northern Ireland's Ulster Transport Authority and the Coras Iompair Eireann (CIE) of the Irish Republic, and assets including locomotives and rolling stock were divided between the two undertakings. The 4-4-0 'Class V' locos were split between the companies thus, locos Nos 83 *Eagle*, 86 *Peregrine* and 87 *Kestrel* were allocated to the UTA in the north and No 84 *Falcon* and 85 *Merlin* to the CIE in the south. The letters 'UT' or 'CIE' being stencilled on the locos' buffer beams.

The ex GNR system was decimated by closures of the majority of its northern routes in the late 1950s, an act which had a knock-on effect for the CIE as many of the old GNR routes shared border crossings with that company. The CIE continued running trains to the stations on the border for a short while after the UTA enforced closures but eventually being starved of passengers they were left with no choice but to withdraw those services.

Steam operations were discontinued by the CIE in 1963, but that was not so in the north of Ireland. The UTA was replaced in 1967 by a new undertaking Northern Ireland Railways (NIR) who took into stock 23 steam locomotives and famously operated steam until the summer of 1970. The NIR operated the last main line steam locomotives in normal service in Ireland and the British Isles, but that as they say is another story!

GNR 'Class V' 4-4-0 three-cylinder Compound No 86 *Peregrine* pictured on shed at Adelaide Road Belfast on 30 August 1958. This loco was waiting to back down to Belfast Great Victoria Street station in order to work an express to Dublin via Dundalk and Drogheda. Loco No 86 was the last of the UTA-operated compounds to be withdrawn in 1961. David Anderson

GNR 'Class V' three-cylinder Compound 4-4-0 No 84 Falcon pictured at Dundalk loco works in September 1959 while being used as a stationary boiler. In 1958 the German company Heinkel sold the production rights of their Bubble Car design to an Irish company and Dundalk Engineering produced what many enthusiasts think was their best ever Bubble Car. An estimated 6486 were made at Dundalk until the final Irish-built car left the former Dundalk Locomotive Works in 1962. David Anderson

GNR 'Class VS' three-cylinder simple 4-4-0 loco No 210 *Erne*, pictured in 1959 at Dublin Amiens Street shed (now Dublin Connolly) as UTA No 59. This class of five engines was introduced in 1948 and built by Beyer Peacock as a development of the 'Class V', all were named after Irish rivers. This engine was withdrawn in 1963. David Anderson

GNR 'S Class' 4-4-0 No 170 *Errigal* is pictured at Dublin Amiens Street in 1959; the loco was then ex Dundalk Works. The name was given when the engine was first introduced in 1913, but removed in 1930 and then reinstated in 1939. This loco was the last of the class to receive the popular blue and scarlet livery. Loco No 170 was withdrawn by the GNR in 1963 and sold to the UTA who then operated it for two more years before finally withdrawing it in 1965, UTA No 170N. David Anderson

GNR 'SG2 Class' 0-6-0 loco No 180 is pictured under the shed clock at Dundalk depot. Built by Beyer Peacock in 1915 this loco was transferred to the CIE in 1958 (note stencilling on the buffer beam) being withdrawn in 1961. David Anderson

GNR 'Q Class' 4-4-0 loco No 132 is pictured at Dundalk Depot in September 1959.
Built by Neilson Reid in 1901 the loco was rebuilt in 1922 (becoming Qs Class), it was
transferred to the CIE in 1958 and withdrawn in 1961. The loco is seen in very clean
condition and when acting as 'in steam' standby loco. David Anderson

GNR 'S2 Class' 4-4-0 No 190 *Lugnaquilla* is pictured 'on shed' at Adelaide, Belfast in 1958. This loco was built by Beyer Peacock and introduced in 1915; it was one of a series of GNR engines which were named after Irish mountains. The loco was transferred to the UTA (becoming No 62) in 1958 and withdrawn in 1965. In December 1945 the loco was involved in a fatal accident while hauling the noon Belfast-Dublin express. The driver and an inspector were killed after a coupling rod broke away at speed and punctured the loco's boiler. David Anderson

GNR 'RT Class' 0–6–4T No 166 (later UTA No 24) is pictured at Belfast, Adelaide on 30 August 1958. Built in 1911 by Beyer Peacock this was one of a series of four engines with low boiler fittings for use on the Belfast Dock railway system, which had a restricted tunnel under the Queens Bridge. Alongside are two GNR 'U Class' 4-4-0s. David Anderson

With the closure of many Ulster Transport Authority lines and the introduction of the new 'WT Class' 2-6-4T class between 1946 and 1950 the older NCC engines were gradually withdrawn from traffic. Showing many Midland Railway characteristics 'V Class' 0-6-0 No 15 is pictured at Belfast York Road depot in UTA black 'lined out' livery, on 1 September 1959. Note the ancient appearance of the tender with outside springing and rear located number plate. This loco survived in service until 1961. David Anderson

Pictured at Belfast Adelaide shed on 1 September 1959 is 'W Class' 2-6-0 No 97 *Earl of Ulster*, built 1935 and withdrawn in 1965. In Northern Ireland the Northern Counties Committee (NCC) main lines served Larne, Ballymena, Coleraine, Portrush and Londonderry from Belfast York Road station. The system was revolutionised in 1933 by the introduction of the first of the Derby-designed 'W Class' engines, a design which made use of several standard LMS features. The first four of the 15 engines in the class were built at Derby and the remainder were assembled at Belfast York Road Works using the parts shipped to the NCC by LMS Derby. The engine pictured is fitted with a cabside tablet catcher and is coupled to a larger Stanier 3500-gallon/7-ton tender. David Anderson

Chapter 10

FREIGHT ICON – NER RAVEN 'Q6'

As a general increase in freight traffic was experienced throughout the UK at the beginning of the 20th century and the demands on steam motive power depots grew, new locomotives were urgently needed. The North Eastern Railway met their need for a reliable and robust freight locomotive, to handle growing coal and mineral traffic, by adopting a 1913 design from the office of their then Chief Mechanical Engineer Vincent Lichfield Raven, who later became Sir Vincent Raven.

Born in Norfolk, Raven first joined the NER at Gateshead in 1876. His distinguished engineering career included a spell between 1915 and 1919 at the Royal Arsenal, Woolwich and the Admiralty. Thereafter Raven returned to the NER but resigned in 1922, before the formation of the London North Eastern Railway. In 1923 he became Technical Advisor to the LNER and simultaneously a director of the once-famous engineering company Metropolitan Vickers. Raven, who retired from work in 1925, died while on holiday in Felixstowe in 1934. However a Raven connection with the LNER continued as his daughter Guendolen (one of four children) had chosen to marry a locomotive engineer, one Edward Thompson of LNER 'B1' fame.

The LNER Raven 'Q6' class (NER 'T2' class) owed much in its design features to an earlier Worsdell NER 0-8-0 freight locomotive the 'Q5' class (NER 'T' and 'T1' class). The North Eastern Railway 'Q6' class total was 120 engines which were delivered in six batches between 1913 and 1921. After grouping (1923) they carried the LNER number series 3340 to 3409 (built Darlington Works) and 3410 to 3459 (built by Armstrong Whitworth & Co

Ltd); British Railways numbers allocated in 1948 were 63340 to 63459. In traffic the superheated two-cylinder 'Q6' engines (power classification of 6F) were an instant success and worked all over the NER system originally being allocated to depots serving coal mining and areas where heavy industry predominated.

At the time of grouping the 'Q6' locos were allocated to Tyne Dock, Borough Gardens, Blaydon, Carlisle Canal, Stockton, Newport, Darlington, Neville Hill (Leeds), Selby, Dairycoates, and Springhead (both Hull). Members of the class would occasionally be used for medium and long distance freight, as well as the heavy mineral traffic for which they were designed. During LNER ownership, the Q6s tended to venture farther afield including trips to Manchester via the Woodhead route. In the 1940s, they were also observed working as far south as Peterborough and March.

Raven had succeeded in creating a strong and reliable locomotive which gave good service right up to the end of BR steam. Because of their success the class remained mainly unmodified, although to keep in line with steam engineering progress the original Schmidt superheaters were replaced with units of a Robinson design from about 1930 onwards and the boilers were updated to LNER 50A types. The 50A boilers had their steam domes set 1ft 3in further back than the original NER Diagram 50 boilers and because their design incorporated a sloping firebox throat plate new tubes were fitted.

The Q6s had no train-braking ability, but they did have a single brake cylinder which operated the brakes on the tender and locomotive. The preserved example No 63395 when first restored to running condition in 1970 had vacuum brake equipment fitted so that it could haul passenger traffic on preserved lines.

No 63395 was the final Q6 to be overhauled at Darlington Works in September 1965 and, along with 63387 of Hartlepool shed, was the last Q6 in service. Following withdrawal, on 9 September 1967, 63395 was moved into store at Tyne Dock shed pending preservation.

*NELPG was formed in 1966 with the intention of preserving some of the steam locomotives still working in the North East of England. In the first 18 months the ambitious volunteers had raised sufficient funds to purchase two heavy freight locomotives, J27 0-6-0 No 65894 and Q6 0-8-0 No 63395. In 1972 the group was donated another locomotive from the North East, mixed traffic K1 2-6-0 No 62005. In 1979 NELPG was offered the Q7 0-8-0 No

63460, on long term loan by the National Railway Museum, and in 1983 they purchased J72 0-6-0 tank engine 69023 'JOEM'. In the late 1987s the Group took charge of A2 Pacific 60532 'Blue Peter' on long-term loan. For more info visit www.nelpg.org.uk

In full cry, preserved ex North Eastern Railway Q6 0-8-0 No 63395 pictured in January 2009 at the Great Central Railway during a freight train photo charter. David Gibson

The way it was! Preserved 'Q6' 0-8-0 No 63395 waits in the platform at Loughborough on the GCR, note the 51A shed plate indicating that the loco's home shed was Darlington. January 2009. David Gibson

Raven 'Q6' 0-8-0 6F No 63355 is pictured during a 1960 visit to Darlington Works. This loco was built at Darlington and first entered service in May 1913, it was withdrawn in July 1963; note also the cab end of No 63391, another Darlington-built engine. The class can easily be distinguished from the similar-in-appearance Raven 'Q7' 0-8-0s (introduced during the same period) by the fact that the outside cylinders on the Q6 drove on the third pair of driving wheels, while the 'Q7' loco cylinders drove on the second pair. Author's collection

The train consists of a rake of steel mineral wagons commonly called 'windcutters', a name given to the fast moving coal trains which used to be common on the GCR in the steam era, they are in effect British Railways 16-ton mineral wagons. January 2009. David Gibson

This going away shot shows the 'windcutter train' approaching Quorn Station on the GCR, note the tarpaulin sheet which has been rigged between the engine cab roof and the loco tender in order to shelter the footplate crew from the elements. January 2009. David Gibson

Waiting in Platform 2, ex North Eastern Railway 'Q6' 6F 0-8-0 No 63395 (BR number) the loco carried NER No 2238 and LNER number 3395. The 'Q6' class were unglamorous freight workhorses that plied the tracks of the North East of England for 50 years; they were one of the very few pre-Grouping steam locomotives to survive right up to the end of BR steam. January 2009. David Gibson